BELT AND ROAD
INITIATIVE

BELT AND ROAD INITIATIVE

EMERGING WORLD ORDER

TALAT AYESHA WIZARAT

PARTRIDGE

To order additional copies of this book, contact
Toll Free +65 3165 7531 (Singapore)
Toll Free +60 3 3099 4412 (Malaysia)
orders.singapore@partridgepublishing.com

www.partridgepublishing.com/singapore

Dedicated to the loving memory of
my parents Begum Aisha Wizarat
and Major (Dr) Wizarat ullah khan
who have been a source of
inspiration and pride
for me.

CONTENTS

ACKNOWLEDGEMENTS

To pursue any activity particularly academic endeavour one needs mental stimulation which comes from reading, discussion and debate. Another source of motivation is provided by the family whose love and care is indispensable.

I have been lucky to enjoy both sources of motivation. In January 2021 my teaching contract ended, I was a bit disappointed. At this stage my daughters Hira Khan and Namra Khan advised me to focus on writing my book, which I had always dreamt of doing but could not due to teaching responsibility. I am very grateful to them and my son-in-law Jahanzeb Khalid for their support and care. My husband Lt. Col (Retd) Mohammad Tahir has also been very supportive. My siblings Dr Shahida Wizarat, Ms Zakia Wizarat Mrs Yasmin Arshad and Mr Nusrat ullah khan have also been a source motivation. Dr Shahida guided me throughout publication process and Zakia was helpful in editing the volume. My nephew and Research Assistant Asad U.Khan provided full support to me. My neice Kanza believes that people who provide emotional support are as important as others so thanks Kanza Khan and nephew Basharat

U.Khan. My nephews Ali Arshad and Talha Arshad also deserve my gratitude. Another person who was supportive is Siraj Ahmed Sabki who joined me as house help but proved to be useful in taking care of my research documents and typing work.

I would also like to thank the scholars who invited me to their seminars, foreign and Pakistani scholars and experts who gave me the opportunity to interview them. Mr Naveed Hassan Khan Ex-Education Attaché Pakistan Embassy Beijing, China also deserves special mention for his help and support. My countless number of friends living all along the Karakoram Highway and Gwadar also deserve my thanks and gratitude. The library staff of all the centres of learning I visited also deserve special thanks for helping me.

PREFACE

As a child I used to hear tales about life on the Silk Road in ancient times. Like all stories these were romanticised versions of reality, they presented exciting and highly stimulating scenarios. Many years later I decided to visit the area in order to interact with people living in the region. It is a well-known fact that some companions of the prophet (peace be upon him) left Arabia after his death, they went all the way to China to learn special skills for which China was famous and to preach the new religion.

When President Xi Jinping presented Belt and Road Initiative in 2013 it aroused immediate interest of countries in Asia and Africa. Many European states also watched the situation with interest. US was a bit apprehensive looking upon this as an emerging challenge. Many people including scholars consider BRI to be part of China's efforts to revive the Silk Road. In reality BRI is going to be much more than a set of trade routes. The concept of 'economic corridor' is far more multi-dimensional. These inter-connected economic corridors will be provided with modern infrastructure, industrial centres and agricultural ventures.

BRI is designed to promote academic cooperation between universities of member countries. Training of young faculty and development of academic programmes in keeping with needs of the society is also planned. In some regions of the world water management and storage of this scarce asset is dire need of the society. In other cases some other aspect could be more important. The main idea is to promote cooperation and learn from each other.

The idea of creating Digital Silk Road (DSR) is rather new. Work has already begun on this project, it is expected to provide better means of communication between member states. Modernisation of communication systems is crucial for military security, promotion of trade and poverty alleviation. Industrial ventures would lead to creation of jobs and other benefits. Creation of Special Economic Zones and Industrial Parks would create environment conducive for industrial development. China is planning to transfer some of its industries to overseas locations, this could open up opportunities for some developing states.

The Chinese model of development is gradually becoming popular among Asian and African countries. The factors behind this growing interest are being explored as the Chinese have done little to project their model of development. The most important reason appears to be China's spectacular rise right before our eyes. It broke the cycle of poverty and joined the ranks of developed states.

According to a World Bank report China has pulled 800 million people out of grinding poverty. In 1981 poverty afflicted 88 percent of the population but in 2015 it had come down to 0.7 percent. This is no small achievement; it offers hope to poverty-stricken people all over the third world. Chinese model has an appeal for developing states, but they should not lose sight of the fact that there is no substitute for hard work, honesty effective planning and efficient management.

My book 'Belt and Road Initiative: Emerging World Order' is designed to understand the importance of this venture. If BRI succeeds in creating a new pattern of economic and political interaction between developed states and the third world, it will result in the emergence of a new world order. Before making an attempt to define the various dimensions of the emerging world order we must discuss the existing world order in some detail.

The present world order was imposed by the victor nations after the end of World War II. Although the colonial era was drawing to an end the states aspiring for independence lacked a strong voice. The bipolar system tilted in favour of Western states led by the US. The UN was heavily influenced by the developed states particularly the US that also controlled the IMF, World Bank and other instruments of economic power. Even after the process of decolonisation was completed in the political realm, the economic relationship between ex-colonies and colonial powers remained intact.

There are innumerable examples of this but two appear to be more significant.

1. France imposed a special tax on fourteen of its ex-African colonies on the pretext of having developed their infrastructure. They are also required to keep their surplus foreign currency funds and gold reserves in French banks. All this in spite of the fact that lack of infrastructure has been the main hurdle in their development.

2. The terms of trade offered to developing states (ex-colonies) are extremely adverse as their exports are based on raw materials. They import manufactured goods from developed states (ex-colonial powers). The cost of manufactured goods is much higher and constantly on the rise. There is a net transfer of resources from developing to developed states, leading to prosperity in the West and increasing poverty in Africa and Asia. This suits the developed states and they have no interest in changing the pattern.

The bipolar system was transformed into unipolar with the breakup of Soviet Union. This was seen as a 'triumph' of capitalism. US took full advantage of this, using its military-industrial complex to occupy various countries, in order to establish direct control over the natural resources of these states. The US imposed regimes of its choice on target states like Libya, Iraq and Afghanistan, murdering national leaders and pushing these states into severe turmoil.

According to an article appearing in Express Tribune on 28th February 2022 US has been involved in 102 wars which is 81 percent of all armed conflicts between 1945 and 2001. The US has 750 military bases spread over the entire globe whereas UK has 145, Russia 36 and China only 5.

Alex Ward has stated that the US lost many wars and failed to win an even larger number of conflicts in recent times. Wards analysis of reasons which have led to this development is interesting, but beyond the scope of this book. United State's recent defeat in Afghanistan, and failure to change the regimes in Syria and Iran auger well for the future. Some journalists have also reported, that ISIS and some other terrorist organisations, were also created by the US in order to use them against its adversaries. In this context interview given by Hillary Clinton to a journalist is very revealing.

Keeping in view the current US role in world politics, one can expect that the US is still the strongest military and economic power, and there is little possibility of change in the near future. The US has also been trying to use all the means at its disposal short of war, to destabilise some states on the route of BRI.

However, a growing number of scholars also believe that the era of US dominance is drawing to an end. US hegemony was the result of many factors perhaps the most important being its military power. However, in recent times due to increase in China's military capability the US has declined in comparative terms. The dollar also dominated the world economy for many years, but now a growing number of states are opting for trade in other currencies. China and Russia are ready to trade in their own currencies in order to circumvent the US sanctions. Recently Saudi Arabia has also signed a deal with China which is based on Chinese currency.

US influence in the Middle East has also suffered severe setbacks. Some recent examples are noteworthy; China helped Iran and Saudi Arabia to negotiate their differences and reestablish diplomatic relations. Saudi Arabia and Syria have also agreed to restore diplomatic relations severed many years back. The Syrian president also visited UAE and got warm welcome in Dubai. The Russians are working behind the scene to help Syria and Turkiye to normalise their relations. These developments have enhanced Chinese and Russian influence in the region.

China has overtaken the US in many areas of importance for world economy. It is estimated that between 2030 and 2035 China will emerge as the largest economy inspite of the damage caused by

Covid 19. If BRI gains momentum this development might occur sooner than expected.

The content of the new world order emerging as a result of success of BRI would be shaped by a number of factors. The relationship between China, Russia and states that choose to be part of the frame-work would define the substance of future politics.

Some of the features of emerging world order are already perceptible. It is expected to be based on cooperation rather than conflict. With better infrastructure trade and tourism are expected to grow, resulting in peaceful interaction between nations. Need for weapons would be reduced and demand for items to promote industrial and agricultural development can be expected to grow.

Economic cooperation leads to interdependence. In the past interdependence has resulted in political integration. Two examples in recent years stand out i.e EU and ASEAN. Cooperation like conflict is habit forming. If cooperation is promoted as a policy measure it will lead to further cooperation.

Unlike the present system dominated by one super power the emerging one is expected to be multipolar. The soft power of China is expected to grow further but this should not be taken as a threat by rival states. Zero sum model is losing its significance in view of change in scenario.

The road to prosperity through mutual cooperation is wide open, inviting all the states to join the venture. This could change past pattern of interaction between rival states, reducing the chances of military adventurism under the new world order. The narrative promoted by the US regarding emergence of threat emanating from China, is losing its credibility with the passage of time. The number of states adhering to this concept is expected to decline further in future. Wars have led to dislocation, destruction and poverty. This problem can be overcome only by increasing cooperation and containing conflict.

CHAPTER I

Trade Routes Old and New: Historical and Geostrategic Dimensions

It will not be an exaggeration to say that ancient trade routes played an important role in shaping history. These trade routes to a large extent determined the content of politics of the era and also set the trends for the future. Trading ventures are as old as civilization itself. It is remarkable that even in the absence of modern means of communication, traders were able to launch initiatives which enriched them, while also providing a similar opportunity to their counterparts on the other side of the border.

Trade filled the gaps then as it does now; sources of survival and comfort which were not available to the society could be acquired from other societies, city states and empires. This created interdependence and paved the way for two-way traffic in goods. Cultural barriers had to be

1

broken; geographical barriers were not allowed to stand in the way either. What we know through historical accounts about trading ventures of the past paint the picture of adventurous individuals driven by desire to make profit.

Historical accounts mention 'roads' which were used to trade various items. In reality these 'roads' were just tracks which passed through all kinds of terrain mostly tortuous and difficult to traverse. On these 'roads' or routes cities, towns and other population centres automatically grew. There were 'Sarai' or guest houses where traders could get food and accommodation. There were store houses for the safe keeping of merchandise.

The focus was so much on exchange of goods like silk or tin (which often gave the route its name,) that people overlooked more meaningful and substantive items, which were exchanged eg ideas. When people interacted across borders they exchanged ideas about culture, religion and other matters holding importance for them. Methods of production of goods were often exchanged[1]. Civilizations were enriched as a result of these interactions.

Trade routes have been instrumental in promoting prosperity at regional level and beyond. They served like arteries nourishing political, economic and social interaction between societies falling in their range. The trade routes created more cooperation than conflict, even though some element of competition and conflict did exist. There is historical evidence to suggest, that at times these conflicts were exacerbated, leading to war under certain circumstances. These trade routes presented an intricate network of corridors on land and sea. The terrain they covered was invariably difficult.

Security was a vital part of the entire exercise, it is the subject of a subsequent section, suffice it to say that the task of providing security was taken seriously by the political authorities.

It has often engaged the interest of historians, academicians as well as general public as to how many trade routes existed in antiquity. It is a difficult question to answer firstly, because each trade route was a complex network of 'roads' and tracks. Besides, trade routes existed so long as they were needed but when the need for a certain item ended then the route outlived its utility and vanished. There was a 'slave route'; strong African males were caught off the coast of Africa and sold in Americas, the Caribbean and other areas of the world. The Slavs too were sold as slaves (the term probably can be traced back to the name of enslaved group)[2] The slave women were often good looking. The price depended on looks of the slave women. It was a rather shameful period in human history. However between mid to the end of nineteen century slavery was abolished from much of the world.

Peter Frankopan has discussed in his book the discovery of new lands. Late fifteenth century led to the development of several new routes. With the discovery of America, Spain and Portugal created linkages between this newly discovered land and Europe which were later extended to include Africa and Asia[3]. These routes were different in nature from trade routes like the Silk Road. The Silk Road and other similar ventures were between sovereign entities like city states or empires. There was give and take; both sides had something to offer and the relationship was mutually beneficial. There were ups and downs, often one side's gains were greater than those of the other side, sometimes wars became inevitable resulting in bloodshed.

Gold was discovered in West coast of Africa, tales of riches reached Europe and that led to colonization of the African continent. When America was discovered and colonized more resources including gold started flowing into Europe[4]. The flow of gold was from Africa and America to Europe. In the beginning Britain for its trade with Mughal India used gold to pay for goods. But later Mughal rule was brought to an end and British occupation of India changed the nature of trade between them. On the 'gold route' other items which were part of this network were precious and semiprecious stones. All these items catered to the whims of newly rich Europeans and the emerging population of European colonialists in America[5].

Trade in precious metals has held fascination for people of all continents throughout ages. Gold and silver were much sought after along with pearls and precious stones. Large deposits of silver were found in South America, some were also discovered in North America and Europe.

The Silk Road passed through mountain ranges, plains and sea routes. As already mentioned, it was spread over one of the most inhospitable regions of the world. It started in the Chinese province of Gansu and followed Northwestern course. It split into three parts, two of which rejoined at Kashgar. The third route went north of Tran Shan Mountains to Almaty (Kazakhstan) the route split once again one track leading to Fergana Valley, the other route joining it briefly in the south. One of the routes went to the Caspian Sea or Black Sea from where goods could be carried to various destinations in Europe[6].

The Southern route was a single route beginning in China and passing through Karakoram region into what is now Pakistan. From Gilgit-Baltistan in Northern Pakistan it passed through what is now Khyber Pakhtunkhwa (KP) province of Pakistan, proceeding to Baluchistan province, it touched on Khorasan (Iran) and onwards to Mesopotamia (modern Iraq) travelling all the way to Turkiye. Another branch passed through Northern Pakistan into Afghanistan, Iran and then following the land route to Syria. From Turkiye and Syria goods were transported to various European destinations through the sea route[7].

Other routes starting in Western China went southward to Tibet, India, Burma (Myanmar) and other Southeastern states. Separate shorter routes also starting in China went directly to Vietnam and other East Asian states. For a long time, Silk was the main item traded through these trade routes. However, after Chinese monopoly over silk trade ended other items took the place of silk[8].

Another silk route corridor beginning in East Asia passed through several political entities coinciding with modern day Vietnam, passing through Strait of Malacca it reached Indonesia, India, Sri Lanka, Pakistan, Iran, Iraq, Syria, Turkiye, Egypt, Italy and other European destinations. All These tracks were spread over land and maritime routes[9].

The actual silk route was spread over more than seven thousand miles. The distance travelled over the seas was in addition to this. Silk Road connected all major regions of the world, creating livelihood for thousands of people all over the world. There were times when Silk Road was closed down for various reasons which will be discussed in detail later but the interesting thing is that it was always revived. There are some other interesting aspects of ancient Silk Road which I came to know while working on this book. Even to this day people talk of the Silk Road spirit. Political entities through which the Silk Road passed are believed to have been imbued with a certain spirit or approach which was common between them. The President of China Mr Xijinping used the term in several of his interviews and statements. There are some skeptics who regard the term to be rather romanticized version of reality. Another aspect which is of interest to me is the story telling tradition along the Silk Road cities and towns. Many cities sprang up along this important artery of world commerce. When traders, scholars and travelers passed through these cities they entertained themselves by various means one of which was story telling. In one or two places the tradition has survived to this day[10].

Another important item traded was spices of various types. The 'Spice route' began at the Western coast of Japan, it included China and Indonesian islands[11]. Passing through Strait of Malacca to Sri Lanka and Southern tip of India. It reached Middle East from where it was connected to Europe. The route was spread over 15000 kilometers. Cinnamon from Sri Lanka and Cassia from China reached Middle East. The 'spice route' largely coincided with 'Maritime Silk route' cloves, cardamom, coriander, cumin seeds, turmeric, mustard, ginger and pepper (black, white and green) and saffron were some popular spices which gave food special flavour.

Spice trade was highly profitable and Arab merchants played important role as 'middle men'. The European urge to find a direct route to spice producing areas is well known, particularly as it led to discovery of Americas. Discovery of America was accidental but ultimately the Europeans found the 'direct route' they were looking for. The Europeans wanted to remove the Arab merchants who had been an important link in the chain, ultimately they succeeded in achieving their objective. It caused immense problems for Arab merchants and their economic interests. All the profits from this trade started going to European merchants. It also paved the way for colonization of spice producing regions. The European powers had tough competition among them for control over the spice route.

The competition led to inter-state wars for control of this trade route mostly among European powers. The twentieth century wars of liberation launched by the colonized people led to their independence, but economic domination by ex-colonial powers continues even to this day. The pattern of interaction between nations changed and is now a part of history.

Another important trade route was 'salt road', in many ways salt is regarded to be an essential link in survival of human beings. Humans discovered various uses of salt around 5000 to 10,000 years back. It started being used to preserve food particularly meat and fish; the use of this technique made a big difference enabling communities to reduce the occurrence of famine for example. This discovery was followed by an increase in world population.

Salt has two major sources, it can be extracted from salt mines which occur in nature. Technology is needed to extract salt from the mines. In ancient times methods existed which would now be considered crude. Technology for the purpose of developing salt mines has undergone tremendous changes in the last two centuries. Oceans and lakes having a high content of salt are also seen as sources of salt. Water is collected and allowed to evaporate leaving salt behind.

Ancient civilizations were often founded near salt deposits and abundant water resources like rivers or oceans. In ancient times Sahara desert was an important link in salt trade, since other parts of West Africa were not rich in salt. Transported via camel caravans and boats along rivers like Niger and Senegal, salt reached markets to be sold or exchanged for much needed goods like ivory, hides, copper, iron and cereals [12]. Other regions engaging in salt trade were spread over some parts of Asia and Europe. Salt was also used as currency to buy slaves which led to use of term 'not worth his salt'. Another term also shows the importance of salt at least in some cultures where loyalty to salt is an essential expectation. People who share salt (by inviting people to lunch or dinner) are considered to have made great favour. All those who benefit from this gesture are supposed to show their gratefulness. This was a tradition which is almost extinct now.

Experts talk about 'water wars' which could occur in future. Oil wars have taken place, one example of this is US aggression against Iraq in 1991 and 2003. The young people in the West who demonstrated against the two wars of aggression were convinced that it was only to occupy Iraqi oil[13]. It might come as a surprise to some that in ancient times many wars were fought for salt and were lost due to lack of it. In the eighteenth century when war was launched to drive Britain out of America Benjamin Franklin made a secret deal with Bermuda for the supply of salt. Salt was an important source of revenue for governments as it constituted a major economic asset.

Pakistan is a major producer of salt. The Khewra Salt mines are an important source of pink salt in the world. There are some forty types of salts in the world of which pink salt is supposed to have special qualities. Somehow Pakistan continues to provide India with pink salt at a throw away price. India sells this under the title of 'Himalayan Salt,' and is believed to be making huge profits from this salt trade[14].

It is believed that Alexander and his soldiers discovered that their horses were often found licking the rocks that lead to the discovery of Khewra salt mines. Under the Mughal rule the mines were developed to generate financial resources.

Pakistan and some other salt producing countries are using these sites as tourist attraction which is a source of revenue. About 240,000 tourists visit Khewra salt mines every year. There are college and university students and general public among Pakistani tourists. Apart from this a large number of foreign tourists also visit the mines. One special feature of these visits is the health related dimension. Some among the visitors believe that breathing inside the salt mine clears their throat and lungs.

Another major trade route was the 'incense route', the incense trade was very profitable. The entire region from Southern Arabian Peninsula (modern day Yemen and Southern Saudi Arabia) all the way to what is now Jordan and Palestine produced incense that had ready market in Europe and South Asia. The Nabateans[15] who had a flourishing civilization played an important role in promoting incense trade. Petra a city on the trade route controlled by Nabateans was also famous for its irrigation system, water management skills and rocks-cut architecture. There were many other towns which sprang-up along the incense road.

The trade in frankincense and myrrh from Southern Arabia and Oman in Persian Gulf to the Mediterranean flourished between 3rd Century to 2nd Century AD. The Incense Route was a network of trade routes spread over more than two thousand kilometers.

It was due to economic power resulting from incense trade, that such a long desert supply route from Arabia to Mediterranean, in Hellenistic-Roman era could be effectively managed. Towns, a large number of forts and caravan Sarai, had to be developed in order to manage and control the trade route. The trade route shifted twice due to earthquakes, the first of which was in AD 363 and the second in AD 551. These earthquakes caused tremendous damage and destruction leading to abandonment of the route. There were two routes one leading to the west which was changed after the earthquakes. The other moved east ward to China also covering other parts of Asia. The ancient trade caravans carried items like gold, gems, coloured glass etc from West to East. East provided silk, spices, incense and other type of perfumes, ceramics and precious stones to name a few.

Another important trade route was the tea road. Tea produced in China became popular all over Europe due to the cold climatic conditions. Many Asian countries also developed liking for Chinese tea. There were two main tea roads, one going from tea producing Chinese province of Yunnan to Middle East and Europe. The other going east which further bifurcated, one branch took tea to parts of South Asia and the other covered East and Southeast Asia. The third branch is known as tea-horse road. For more than a thousand years a major artery of commerce connected Sichuan (China) to Lhasa in Tibet.

It was a mountain track spread over 2,250 km. Chinese porters both men and women carried heavy loads over thousands of miles. It took them a long time to reach their destination. Main mode of transportation, however, were animals. On this historical trade route Chinese tea was traded for Tibetan horses. It has been stated that the price of a horse was 60 kg of tea (Michael S. Yamashita / National Geographic Stock.) [16] Tea was popular in Tibet for several reasons but two standout. Firstly, cold climate which was particularly harsh during winter months created demand for tea. The other factor was that monks and priests, wanted to keep awake at night, in order to worship their deities.

If tea was important for Tibetans, horses were equally important for the Chinese. Holding a large country together and providing efficient governance required quick means of communication. In the absence of modern means of communication, horses were the only available alternative. Proper governance and security of the state depended on a number of complex factors, one of which was quick mode of communication and decision making.

Tin trade has been important for all civilizations. The Bronze Age owes quite a bit to the discovery of safer sources of tin. Tin deposits were spread over only certain regions of the world. Africa, Asia and parts of Europe having deposits of tin, played an important role in trade and commerce of those times. Tin roads criss crossed Europe bringing Iberian tin to Mediterranean region for example. Similarly, trade routes were spread over Africa and Asia. Central Asia was known to have tin deposits and was connected to the tin markets, where they could sell their product. Tin road connected Central Asia to other regions. Another aspect which emerged during my research of trade routes was that routes were not reserved for trade of one item only. Since Silk Road was among the most important trade routes, there are many instances of tin merchants using Silk Road particularly in Central Asia.

The extraction and use of tin dates back to around 3000 BC, which coincides with the beginning of Bronze Age[17]. Copper after being mixed with another metal (eg tin) became harder and the melting point also changed. Knowledge regarding various metals, their extraction techniques and other related matters were kept secret. But there are also instances of sharing this knowledge when required for mutual benefit.

Fur trade was restricted mostly to Canada, what is now US, European states and Russia. Historically for fur trade water routes were the 'natural highways' traversed by traders and other people associated with the trade[18].

It was a highly profitable venture dominated by the Europeans particularly the Dutch, French and the British played an important role. The European powers were mainly competing against each other in the fur business but another major item was fish. The European fisherman were familiar with the rich fish resources further west on the Atlantic coast. Cod was popular in Europe. Cleaning their fish on land took several weeks which made it necessary to evolve peaceful relations with the local people.

The types of fur available were beaver fur (for making hats), fancy furs like mink and various other types. The Fur industry attracted attention of European powers, Russia and the European settlers. The settlers pursued their own economic interests, which often clashed with those of the colonial governments and, of course the indigenous people. These people were an important link in the Fur trade as they brought the fur and hides to European traders who had warehouses and storage facilities. The European traders operated from special centres called 'trading posts'. All over the trade route European powers-maintained trading posts and warehouses[19].

There was intense competition at all levels, between European states, in which European powers used their local allies, thus dividing the indigenous population. The companies (from different countries) like HBC, NWC and Russian fur companies also had cut throat competition among them. The tussle was focused on acquiring full control over natural resources of the indigenous people.

Companies competed with companies and countries with countries. Missionaries were brought in to convert the local people, who were interested in trading with the West but, not in their religion. Ultimately the local people were the only losers as they were colonized and deprived of their resources. Of the several wars fought by the European powers against each other, the local people became cannon fodder. Wars were not the only cause of death and destruction. There were outbreaks of diseases, climatic factor and other reasons as well.[20]

Amber road was a major trade route connecting Europe with North Africa and other parts of the world. Amber was a popular gem, the colour of amber ranges from various shades of yellow, orange and brown. There are some red varieties too. Around 3000 BCE amber produced in Baltic region was carried to various parts of Europe and beyond. Traders and travelers carried amber through interconnected routes intersecting the Silk and Salt roads. Under the ancient Roman period Amber Road ran vertical from Venice and Rome all the way to St Petersburg. Various sub routes reaching Asia and Africa branched out from the main route[21]. The term 'Amber road' was coined by Cambridge University archaeologist Jose Maria de Navarro in 1920, to refer to an interconnected set of trails, connecting the Baltic and Adriatic during ancient times.

Revival of interest in historical trade routes had focused attention on the question, whether the idea is feasible in the light of many political and technological changes, which have taken place in the last few centuries? It is a documented historical fact that at least on three occasions the land Silk route fell into disuse due to introduction of new technologies[22]. Political exigencies also affected developments leading to diversion of trade routes[23].

It is argued here that four factors are crucial in determining whether a route can be revived:

Firstly, in view of the fact that empires of the past have vanished giving rise to nation states the political scenario presents new realities. It is also true that some of these states suffer from political instability and a legacy of interstate disputes. These realities make it more difficult for the adversaries to come together or give geographical, economic or political access to their rival states. Mutual suspicions stand in the way of cooperation. To the extent that the regional states are able to overcome animosities they will be ready to take calculated risks for mutual benefit. One cooperative step could lead to more, bringing prosperity to the entire region. This analysis might appear to be rather optimistic to some readers but it is politically feasible inspite of inherent difficulties.

Secondly, providing security to the trade route could be another major challenge. Non-state actors on their own accord or as proxies of regional or global powers, could act to stop the revival of an old trade route. It will be vital for the revival of old trade routes or launching of new ones that states involved in the venture coordinate security arrangements.[24]

Thirdly, technology and its role cannot be overlooked. It is vital that means of communication are not only developed but also that they are economically feasible. In the words of Erich Stake rail is much faster than sea transport and much cheaper compared to air freight[25]. Although the significance of geography has been somewhat reduced as a result of technological innovation, it would not be realistic to conclude that geography has become irrelevant. The long span of land covering the historical trade routes often followed inhospitable terrain. It is more costly to build the infrastructure in this type of terrain. In case of Silk Route, it will be necessary to use the sea lanes as well as land corridors.

Lastly, assessment is required whether demand for commodities traded in the past exists today. If the pattern of demand has undergone change, it should not be source of worry, as long as interdependence continues. Under the new scenario different set of products might be in greater demand. As a matter of fact, this shift has already taken place.

China, Pakistan, states in South Asia and Europe have become dependent on Middle Eastern oil and gas while European states (including Germany) are importing computers, textiles and other goods rather than silk and perfumes from China[26].

Hopes for the revival of any trade route including the Silk Route would also depend on factors like economic compatibility, affordability and interdependence. An additional requirement is ability of partners to sustain the system.

Lessons from the Past

It is clear that political, strategic and economic environments have undergone tremendous changes over the last few centuries. Inspite of this reality, it would be imperative, to draw lessons from a study of history of various trade routes.

As already stated, most of these routes were spread over long and difficult tracks of land and sea, spanning several empires and city states. It was marked by intense competition between major powers, to establish control over the life lines of world commerce. Those who were able to control them gained immense political influence and economic power, due to their ability to generate revenue, from trade taking place through their territory. A number of cities sprang up all along the trade routes providing services of various kinds to the merchants[27].

Empires often drew their strength from their ability to control trade routes; they could fall or be weakened when trade routes changed their course due to political or technological reasons. When empires were unable to provide protection to the traders and their agents, it invariably resulted in loss of control over the trade routes. The trading empire grew as a result of security and other compulsions. The primary function of this arrangement was protection of not only merchants, their agents and their goods but the maintenance and protection of the trade routes.

The cities along the trade routes provided lodging and dining facilities as well as ware houses for temporary storage of merchandise. The empires collected taxes and security fee, while the cities became prosperous, by providing various services to traders passing through their territories. Trade then, much like today did not enrich only people directly engaging in it, but also people indirectly associated with the process.

The security role of cities was, however, limited; generally, they acted as agents of a superior authority, which could be an emperor or king. Providing security was a complex task requiring not only arms and ammunition but also services of well-trained soldiers and fully fortified fortresses[28].

A study of these routes would bring out several interesting aspects, for example these trade routes were particularly vulnerable to political developments. Since trade routes were major assets, on which depended the livelihood of hundreds of people and, the financial wellbeing of the state no threat could be taken lightly. Those posing threat were either common bandits or political adversaries using bandits and even their own soldiers to disrupt trade. Alliances were frequently formed to maintain the status quo or divert a route in a direction more favorable to the challenger[29]. Political developments were often used to promote expansion or cause diversion of these routes.

The Silk Route became a primary route of trade, it also gave impetus to religious, cultural and social exchanges. The spread of Buddhism and later Islam became possible as a result of these inter civilizational interactions. The prestige enjoyed by Chinese civilization all over Europe and, other regions in ancient times, had many channels but traders contributed the most to the process[30].

The Fur route was important from economic point-of-view but there were complicating factors like national rivalries and animosities. Under this scenario all the powers engaging in Fur trade were constantly in search of new routes for their product. Since Fur trade was very profitable under normal circumstances, resources were generously allocated for developing new Fur routes. In case of other trade routes too states invested resources to find new trade routes.

Revived and New Trade Routes: The Belt and Road Initiative

The Belt and Road Initiative (subject of this book) launched by the Chinese President in 2013 is regarded as an attempt to revive the Silk Road. The BRI tracks closely follow the Silk routes of the past. However, they are much more than revival of past trade routes. The BRI envisages the development and modernisation of infrastructure and creation of opportunities for industrialization of developing states joining BRI. The tracks of BRI are, therefore, much more than trade routes; they encompass an entire system and frame-work to promote economic development in various regions.

CPEC which is one of the tracks of BRI has Karakorum Highway (KKH) as its backbone. It closely follows the ancient Silk Road. KKH has put new life into the ancient Silk Road. While the old Silk Road included tracks used by traders KKH is a modern six track highway. While the ancient Silk Road passed through Pakistan, Iran, Afghanistan, Iraq, Syria and Turkiye from where the traders could continue their journey to Europe, on land or through the maritime route. The difference in the case of CPEC is availability of Gwadar port. Now Chinese imports and exports have direct access to the maritime route thereby reducing the distance and travel time.

The US and India are not favourably disposed to the idea of reviving the ancient Silk Road. India has not joined BRI and it tried to dissuade states like Bangladesh from joining. But it is interesting that Hillary Clinton as US Secretary of State suggested that Pakistan should give India access to Afghanistan and Central Asian states (CAS) under the Silk Road frame-work[31]. Why did the US suggest this knowing well that in view of Pakistan-India animosity it would not be possible. There are only two scenarios, US wanted India to get direct access to Afghanistan and Central Asia to counter balance China and negate BRI. The other dimension could be US desire to reduce Indian dependence on Iran. The US under all circumstances wanted to enhance India's economic and political clout in Afghanistan and Central Asia along with other regions.

Energy Road

A very important new trade route is the oil and gas road. Most of the oil / gas deposits of the world are in the Middle East, Central Asia and Caspian region. Middle East supplies oil and gas to Europe, US, Japan, China, East Asia and South Asia. The Middle Eastern oil reaches Europe, US and Japan through oil/gas tankers. These tankers have to pass through certain choke points i.e Strait of Hormuz, Bab el-Mandeb and strait of Malacca just to name a few. To reduce dependence on these choke points pipelines could become another method of transporting oil. Tankers will carry oil from Middle East to Gwadar from where oil and gas will be carried via pipelines to various points in Xinjiang.

Central Asian oil and gas are carried through pipelines to Europe via Russia but US wanted to bypass Russia and Iran. In this context many ideas were evolved one of which was to carry Central Asian oil/gas through Afghanistan[32], onwards to Pakistan and through the sea route to Europe and Japan. China could get oil directly from Central Asian states through pipelines.

Iran, Pakistan and India (IPI) were working on a proposal to carry Iranian oil for Pakistan and India. IPI pipeline was not acceptable to the US: Under US pressure India wriggled out of the deal. As a pretext to opt out of the deal they asked Iran to lay an underwater pipeline to India by passing Pakistan. They knew well that their demand was economically unfeasible being extremely expensive. Iran has completed the pipeline on its side, but Pakistan has been unable to do so due to paucity of funds according to Pakistani officials.

Another proposal which is still being considered Turkmenistan-Afghanistan-Pakistan-India (TAPI) pipeline[33]. It would have brought oil from Turkmenistan through Afghanistan and Pakistan to India. Pakistan's need for oil would be met besides providing revenues for the pipeline passing through its territory. Surprisingly, this time India did not raise any objections either. After the withdrawal of US forces from Afghanistan, TAPI might become viable and with decline in US clout in the region, Iran-Pakistan-India (IPI) oil pipeline might also gain momentum. Pakistan needs to find safe and cheaper oil for its industrial sector, it would give boost to Pakistan's economy.

Russia is also an important player in the oil/gas sector. It has been supplying these commodities to Europe, however, due to Ukrainian issue and a host of other matters, relations between Russia and Western powers are tense. European powers are dependent on Russian energy sources for part of their needs. North Sea oil cannot meet all their needs, neither is US in a position to do much to help them. Europe is trying to reduce its dependence on Russian gas but has not succeed so far.

An energy pipeline supplying Russian gas to Germany under the name of NORD Stream 2 became the centre of controversy. The US put pressure on European states, to severe their energy linkages with Russia, after the Ukrainian conflict began. Germany's reluctance to take action without prior planning gave rise to discomfort on the part of US. The pipeline was blown up under mysterious circumstances in September 2022.

The major oil and gas suppliers to the world are well known. As far as consumers are concerned there is a long list. China has emerged as a major consumer; it has signed oil deals with some energy rich African states like Nigeria. It has also signed deals with Middle Eastern and Central Asian states[34].

US, Europe and Japan are also major consumers of oil and gas. The US meets more than 60% of its needs from foreign sources, while Europe and Japan are even more dependent on Middle Eastern and other energy rich states.

In South Asia, Pakistan, India and Bangladesh are major consumers. India signed a deal with Bangladesh but clearly the South Asian nation will not be in a position to meet all the needs of India.

To conclude the 'Energy Road', one needs to remember that oil and gas continue to play an important role in world politics, even though alternate sources (solar, wind) have been developed.

Security like in ancient times remains a major issue. The US aggression against Iraq in 1991 and 2003 reflected US desire to control the energy sources of the world. Different reasons were given by the US and European powers for invading Iraq, one of which was Iraqi 'weapons of mass destruction'. In my interviews with experts a professor at a business school, suggested that the main reason behind US desire to occupy Middle Eastern oil and gas deposits, was to cut China off from these sources[35]. According to Western calculations this would delay China's rise as an economic super power. After the failure of this approach the US opted for diplomatic means to delay the rise of China. Pipelines are vulnerable in a number of ways. Any terrorist group can resort to actions like blowing up a pipeline, to put pressure on the government, or catch attention of media. Some of these terrorist groups act as proxies of hostile foreign power[36].

As pointed out earlier the '**Technology Road**' has many tracks and, different technologically advanced nations, enjoy complete monopoly over trade in this area. The rules of trade are controlled by states which transfer technology. The decisions regarding which technology can be provided to which developing state are made almost exclusively by the technology providers. Another distinguishing feature is the role played by multinational corporations. The technology providing states are not a monolithic group; infact there is intense competition between them. Recently US tried to stop Huawei from gaining ground at global level but their efforts were not as successful as they expected. The rules of business applicable to previous roads need to be reevaluated before applying them to 'Technology Road'.

The Arms Silk Road

Most Asian and African countries suffer from security dilemma, they are generally unable to produce their own weapons and have to depend on developed states for arms. Major arms exporting countries include US, UK, France, Germany, Italy and Sweden. Russia is another major source; China too has earned repute as an arms exporter.

Oil producing states of Middle East and Africa, Southeast Asian nations like Indonesia and Malaysia are arms importing states. Pakistan and India also depend on developed countries for their supply of arms. India is being developed as a counter weight to China, all its demands in terms of weapons are met by the West. Pakistan does not regard West to be a secure source of arms as it has been embargoed in the past. A noteworthy feature of arms market is that Pakistan, Turkiye, India, Israel and South Africa are trying to grab a significant proportion of the arms trade. China and Pakistan co-produced JF-17 Thunder Aircraft and Al-Khalid Tank which have a ready market due to their good past performance and lower price tag.

The 'Arms Road' like the ancient trade routes has some specific features: There is tough competition at all levels among arms producing nations. The S-400 produced by Russia has earned reputation as an effective radar system. Turkiye even though a member of NATO has signed a deal with Russia for acquiring S-400. The US has decided to impose sanctions on Turkiye in order to dissuade it from going ahead with the deal. The US wants to make Turkiye more dependent on the West. If Turkiye goes ahead with the deal its dependence on US will decrease in future and other members of NATO might follow this example.

The competition for getting a bigger share of arms market also pervades the Western arms producers. France signed a deal with Australia for providing a certain number of submarines, but after the deal had been signed by the two, UK and US stepped in, offering Australia nuclear powered submarines. The French deal was abandoned by Australia. This episode throws light on many vital aspects of 'arms export' politics. In antiquity alliances could be made or broken to serve one's own interest, for diverting a trade route or developing a new one. Nations competing for sale of arms follow a similar approach in the twenty first century.

When Saudi Arabia showed interest in purchasing JF-17 from Pakistan, US used its clout to dissuade the Arab state, perhaps fearing that an important buyer might drift away in future.

The market is controlled by the arms producers, they earn both wealth and influence. The clout of arms producers keeps increasing, while arms importing nations are at their mercy. They become poorer with the passage of time and inspite of all this the security dilemma continues. There is perpetual competition between arms purchasing nations also, due to which despite spending heavily on arms they remain insecure. The arms producers / exporters are the only ones who gain from this process. 'The military-industrial complex'[37] has become extremely powerful. It is now able to exercise greater influence over domestic as well as foreign policy of the US.

The 'Knowledge Silk Road' is an important aspect of modern life. There can be no progress without creating a knowledge-based society. Since Asian and African countries gained independence the bright among their younger population nurtured ambitions of going to study in a western university. The rich ruling elite also preferred Western university education for their sons and daughters. There were two implications of this policy, firstly the elite ignored the task of establishing high quality centres of higher education within the country.

The more serious implication however, was continuation of Western intellectual domination over the third world. During Soviet era some young people from Asia and Africa went to Soviet universities. This tradition continues even after the end of Soviet era. I know some young people who are studying in Russian universities. Some Chinese universities have acquired high international ranking. Students from developing countries are naturally attracted to these institutions.

There is growing need for collaboration between centres of higher learning among BRI member states. This will fill the knowledge gap between developed and developing states. Linkages with Western universities should continue while enhancing collaboration with Chinese and Russian institutions of higher learning. It needs to be stated however, that developing states need to promote knowledge at national level. Grooming of younger generation for leadership roles in future is the responsibility of civil society.

There is still need for establishing institutions of higher learning in developing states. There has been some progress towards this end in the last few years, but more needs to be done. There is one positive aspect of all this, the civil society will be more balanced having intellectual contribution from many sources instead of just one. China's interest in promoting Knowledge Silk Road through cooperation between universities in BRI countries is designed to fill the intellectual gap.

Iron Silk Road

There is a plan to build a network of railway lines in addition to oil and gas pipelines linking the Middle East to China. 'The Iron Silk Road' would not only closely follow the ancient Silk Road it would further expand it[38]. The railway network would begin in Armenia and end up in Vietnam linking up landlocked states with a large number of port cities. This project although beneficial for all the states, is not free of problems. The greatest hurdle is the difference in economic and political approaches followed by regional states. However, the idea has gained strength since the breakup of Soviet Union, opening up of China, and the globalization of almost all aspects of communication and trade. [39]

Towards the end of 2006 the transport ministers of Asian and other countries signed an agreement to integrate their railway systems. The signatories included Armenia, Azerbaijan, Turkiye, several Central Asian states, Russia, Thailand, Sri Lanka and Vietnam. Other states aspiring to join the process are Pakistan, India, Bangladesh and Singapore. The idea of linking Turkiye with Singapore is several decades old; however, it failed to materialize due to the cold war. This plan of linking Asian railway networks is being developed side by side with the integration of Asian highways which will be standardized.

The scheme of linking Armenia with Vietnam or Turkiye with Singapore, appear to be a bit ambitious in view of the fact, that a large number of states will have to reconcile their differences. But these schemes might become feasible in future and if so, they will bring benefits to all the states particularly the landlocked ones. Instead of creating a parallel network of routes if the scheme is expanded to include Pakistan and China the element of competition will be reduced.

Trains Linking China with Europe

South China Morning Post gave a detailed account of Cargo train link connecting China with Europe[40]. Al Jazeera too gave wide coverage to Iron Silk Road[41] train linking China with UK. New Silk Road Container trains from China to Europe are a regular feature now. Currently the number of trains connecting industrial cities of China with various European cities has increased. A train linking China with Central Asia, Turkiye and various European cities has reduced travel time from one month to twelve days.

Another train connects Beijing with London. It passes through Central Asia and Turkiye finally reaching London. German city of Duisburg is connected to South Western Chinese city of Chongqing (Xinjiang).[42] Similarly Eastern Chinese province of Jiangsu is connected with Hamburg in Germany. The main cargo of this train starting from an industrial hub of China is machinery parts, other manufactured goods and epidemic prevention supplies. The train passes through Kazakhstan, Russia, Belarus, Poland and finally Hamburg. It takes fifteen days to cover 10,000 km journey[43].

The Yiwu-London Railway Line is a freight train it covers 12000 km (7500 miles). It is the second longest railway freight route in the world. The route was opened on 1st January 2017.

The increasing number of trains connecting China with various countries in Europe is one indication of multiplicity of ties between China and Europe. These linkages are growing further with the passage of time. Chinese exports to Europe have increased in the last few years and so have Chinese imports from Europe. China-Europe economic ties are expected to grow further in future.

Another important aspect of Silk Road is the emerging **Digital Silk Road (DSR)**. All the major cities on the Silk Road are being digitally connected to each other through Chinese digital technology. Gwadar, Karachi and Islamabad are being connected to each other and onwards to cities in China. Pakistan will be connected to various corners of the world including Africa, Central, West, East Asia and Europe. In the past Pakistan had to depend on Indian companies for connectivity, but now Chinese companies have under taken the task, of laying under water cables which are more durable. The problem of being disconnected due to political reasons will be minimized.

Jonathan E. Hillman in his book 'The Digital Silk Road' has raised some interesting points but he also reflects inherent distrust of China's long-term goals. A development which can bring the world together and promote peace, is sometimes used by western media to promote competition and conflict. However, the new world order emerging as a result of rise of China, is designed to promote cooperation and strengthen peace. It can bring rival nations on one platform for mutual benefit. It would be unfortunate if Western countries in order to preserve their hegemony try to scuttle BRI.

According to an article in the latest issue of Pakistan Horizon,[44] the author has highlighted a new dimension which has been added to Silk Road. Chinese **Space Silk Road** is a comparatively new phenomenon although the Chinese space programme began in 1960. With the creation of the Chinese National Space Administration in 1993 a major hurdle was crossed. The US Department of Defense (DOD) has accused China of developing 'counter-space weapons' to prevent any attack from an adversary in space. Even if DOD's assessment is correct, it would be a defensive step.

China would put this capability to military use only if a military threat develops in outer space. However, at present China appears to be more interested in economic uses of this technology. Space Silk Road will strengthen Chinese domestic innovation capacity in the industrial sector. It will promote Chinese capability in the field of communication, robotic system, cognitive computing and in many other areas. Chinese Space Laboratory and network of satellites will boost China's role in space related endeavours.

China has offered BRI members to benefit from these resources which would otherwise not be available to them. This is a golden opportunity for BRI member states to benefit from Space Silk Road.

The Politics of Routes and Anti routes

This chapter deals with trade routes and their impact on history and politics. Economic prosperity also depends on trade routes to a large extent. Three types of routes have been discussed in this chapter. Ancient trade routes as we know played an important role throughout history. The second category is of trade routes which existed in the past and have now been revived. The third category is of new routes which have been established in modern era. They owe their existence largely to technological revolution which has transformed the world. There was little need for petroleum and gas in ancient times, but now we have become dependent on these products. Extracting, refining and transporting oil and gas dependent on technology. Whether oil and gas are transported by land route, pipelines or by sea routes these accesses have to be developed. Transportation of some goods by aerial means is more expensive but due to development of technology it is now possible to develop aerial routes.

The task of defining a route is not as difficult now as it was in the past. After a study of history 'route' has been defined as an 'access' or 'passage' on land, sea or air which can be used for trade, travel or any other purpose. Routes are a geographical and political concept which have social and economic consequences. According to Ispahani, routes are 'both an end and a means[45]. Jean Gottman has been quoted to have said access has been a central problem in human history'[46]. Another important concept is 'anti-route'. An 'anti-route' can be a natural or artificially created hurdle to block a route or access. Creating anti-routes can also carry serious consequence.

A study of history shows that geographical barriers seldom deterred people, had that been the case there would have been no Silk Road. Another historical example was the signing of an agreement between Egyptians and Lihyanites which resulted in changing a route to suit the Egyptians. It also resulted in creating an anti-route for their rival power. Most of the wars were fought in history either to maintain control over a route or to change a route by creating an anti-route.

Coming to more recent times when Pakistan and China decided to construct an all-weather road (KKH) they were building a route to further consolidate their friendship. Herman Kreutzmann in his article written some years back examined the social and economic consequences of KKH for the people of Hunza and other Northern Areas of Pakistan. The newly created 'route' had positive impact on the lives of common people[47].

Regarding the creation of sea routes the role of Gwadar is interesting. The US believes that direct access to Indian Ocean will enhance China's ability to protect the sea lanes, important for its oil and gas supplies in case of a threat to them. Other Chinese commercial interests for example its vast trade will also be better protected. The Chinese could also use this opportunity to increase their influence in the region. They would be much less dependent on the good will of other states, for the protection of China's major commercial interests. In the context of US pursuit of containment of China, the access acquired by China to Gwadar becomes even more significant. Should the US try to practice a new version of containment policy, China will be in a better position to handle the challenge. It is with this end in view that China has designed the 'String of Pearls' policy[48].

There are number of examples from current history which show the significance of anti-routes. In fact creating anti-routes is as common as creating routes. There can be different perceptions regarding Indian policy of building Chahbahar port in Iran. On the face of it, it appears to be an attempt to by pass Gwadar. India believed it will be able to convince Afghanistan and Central Asian states to rely on Chahbahar rather than Gwadar. After withdrawal of US forces from Afghanistan Indian plans have suffered a setback. A matter of concern for Pakistan is India's desire to use Chahbahar as a terrorist-cum-spy base for destabilizing Pakistan. If India succeeds then CPEC which is a 'route' will be disrupted by creating an anti-route[49].

The politics of creating routes and anti-routes will become more intense in coming years. It could carry serious consequences for regional and international peace. US and India in particular have openly opposed BRI and its flag ship project CPEC. Both these powers have apprehensions regarding rise of China. Now with China on the verge of becoming largest economy leaving US behind, regional and global rivalries for trade routes might further intensify.

The politics of routes and anti-routes has been in existence for centuries but it has taken a new turn due to introduction of technology. Cooption or neutralization of actors trying to oppose revival of trade routes are two options available for now. Both these approaches carry their own price tags; cooption can work if the other side has the capacity to make a meaningful contribution to the process of integration in the long run, however, neutralization may be more viable in other cases[50].

Chapter I

1 Production of 'tin bronze' travelled from one region to another. Ideas about production methods could also be stolen like Chinese silk production secrets were stolen by Europeans which ended Chinese monopoly over the silk trade.

2 Peter Frankopan, The Silk Roads A New History of the World, London Bloomsbury 2016. P117.

3 Ibid P.202

4 Julie Jones, 'Gold of the Indies', Metropolitan Museum of Art Oct 2002. https://www.metmuseum.org

5 Africa with all its gold remained poor and deprived of facilities while Europe thrived.

6 For details see 'Trade Routes' by Pilar Quaezzaire-Belle, 21 July, 2010 http://world-geography.org/674-trade-routes.htlm

7 Quaezzaire-Belle

8 The Byzantine emperor sent two monks to China, they hid the eggs of silkworms in hollow bamboos. The West stole Chinese secret thus ending Chinese control of silk trade in 552 CE.

9 See Old World Trade Route Projects, http://www.ciolek.com/

10 Kisakhani Bazar in Peshawar was well known for the story telling tradition.

11 To the northeast of Indonesia are a group of islands Moluccas, Malaku and some others which were called 'spice islands', they too were an important source of spices.

12 The Salt Trade of Ancient West Africa, World History Encyclopedia http://www.worldhistory.org

13 Their major slogan was 'no blood for oil'

14 Subject of a lot of discussion in social media in Pakistan where people are questioning the wisdom of this one sided deal. So far the government has

not given a satisfactory response.

15 An ancient Arab tribe living in close proximity to modern day Jordan were astute businessmen and engineers. The ruins of their civilization bear testimony to these skills. They had close interaction with Greeks. http://www.history.com

16 Asia's ancient Tea Horse Road. http://national-geographic.cafepress.com

17 http://www.history.com

18 James A. Ogilvy, 'Fur Trade Routes' published online, last edited on December 5th 2019. p.1

19 John E. Forster and William John Eccles, 'Fur Trade in Canada' updated by Richard Foot and Michelle Felice. Published online last edited 1st November 2019. pp 2-3

20 A mass grave of children was discovered in Canada. They were victims of European policy of compulsory Western education at boarding schools run by missionaries. It was common for indigenous children to be mistreated by missionaries.

21 Jennifer Bilock 'Follow the Ancient Amber Road,' 28th August 2019. The author of the article is a Travel Correspondent.

22 With introduction of bigger and faster ships carrying goods through sea routes became cheaper therefore more popular.

23 Various Islamic Empires at different times in history controlled parts of these trade routes. Western rulers were generally eager to by-pass Islamic land routes as far as possible.

24 States like Pakistan and Iran suffering from political unrest sponsored by political adversaries in their provinces of Baluchistan can coordinate through exchange of intelligence etc.

25 Erich Stake http://uk.news.yahoo.com/silk-road-rail-chinas-factories-220949294. Html#8VLbp6x

26 Erich Stake

27 Trade Routes between Europe and Asia during Antiquity, http://www.metmuseum.org/toah/hd/trade/hdtrade.htm

28 Trade Routes between Europe and Asia during Antiquity.

29 Ptolemy II Philadephus Emperor of Egypt made an alliance with the Lihyanices to secure the incense route. As a result of this alliance trade was rerouted from Dedan to the coast along the Red Sea to Egypt. The competition in the north resulted in Syro-Ephraimite war. Invention of ships popularized sea routes resulting in abandonment of some land routes.

30 The spread of Islam in South East Asia was also due to trade ties. Muslim traders from Middle East maintained high standards of honesty in that era which impressed people they interacted with leading to acceptance of their values and religion.

31 Hillary Clinton's speech made in Chennai India. Dawn 10th May 2012.

32 Now that US has been forced to withdraw its troops from Afghanistan the US might not be interested in this project.

33 Rafael Kandiyoti *Pipelines Flowing Oil and Crude Politics*, (New York IB Tauris 2008) P. 109. The US preferred this project as it would bypass Iran and the project would go to some US oil company. US also preferred other Trans-Afghanistan-Pipelines when Afghanistan was under US occupation.

34 Christopher Davidson, *The Persian Gulf and Pacific Asia From Indifference to Interdependence*, (London: Hurst and Company 2010) P48.

35 Dr Khan a graduate of a leading US university with many years teaching and research experience.

36 Oil and gas pipelines in Baluchistan province of

Pakistan were attacked many times. Responsibility was accepted by insurgents like BLA who according to intelligence agencies are being financed by RAW.

37 The term is normally used to describe the prevailing situation in the US. President Eisenhower used the term in his farewell speech on 17th January 1961 in order to warn the nation of serious consequences of the situation.

38 Erich Stake opcit

39 Ibid

40 South China Morning Post 9th September 2013, http://www.scmp.com Also see 'Iron Silk Road' is still a slow train to Leads, Guardian 24th August 2010. See 'Weaving a New Silk Road' by Ed Blanche, The Middle East, 2009, P3.

41 Al Jazeera 3rd August 2008

42 Xinhua, 28th November 2020.

43 http://www.xinhuanet.com

44 Amna Kalhoro Chinese Space Silk Road: wisions and actions, Pakistan Horizon vol 75, No 4, oct 2022

45 Mehnaz Z. Ispahani *Roads and Rivals the Politics of Access in the Borderlands of Asia*, (London: I B Tauris Co Ltd 1989) Pp 2

46 Ibid

47 Herman Kreutzmann, 'Challenge and Response in the Karakoram: Socioeconomic Transformation in Hunza, Northern Areas', Pakistan Mountain Research and Development, vol 13, No1. (Feb 1993) pp19-39. Also see K. J Miller, The International Karakoram project 1980: A First Report, The Geographical Journal, vol 147, No2. (July 1981) pp 153_163

48 Shannon Jiezzi, The Maritime Silk Road VS the String of Pearls, The Diplomat, 13th February 2014, http://thediplomat.com/2014/02/the-maritime-silk-

road-vs-the-string-of-pearls/

49   As already mentioned earlier, India's serving naval officer kulbhushan Jadhav working for RAW was caught red handed in Pakistan. He entered through Chahbahar under false name of Mubarak Hussain.

50   Talat A. Wizarat, Reviving Historical Trade Routes: A Case Study of the Silk Route-Gateway to China, *Strategic Studies* vol 34 and 35, Winter 2014 and Spring 2015, Number 4 and 1.

Belt and Road Initiative: The Silk Road Economic Belt

The Silk Road Economic Belt (SREB) is the land component of BRI.[1] It envisages a network of trade routes with all the facilities like roads, bridges railway tracks along with storage facilities. However, SREB is much more than just a network of trade routes, it is a whole package including industrial parks, Special Economic Zones and educational cities all over the regions which constitute SREB. The digital dimension of BRI should not be underestimated. Modernisation of digital communication has made communication easier and faster within BRI frame work. Air ports and sea ports have been modernized and some of these facilities have been developed from scratch.

SREB concept is a Chinese idea, it's an attempt to replicate Chinese success in economic sector in other countries. There is a Chinese saying that if you want to be rich built roads. It was possible for

China to make spectacular progress in economic field after their leadership focused on development of infrastructure and proclamation of reforms. As a result, China has pulled eight hundred million people out of poverty. China has a GDP of USD 14.72 trillion (2020). In 2011 it emerged as the second largest economy at global level. There are several studies to suggest that if it's economy continues to grow at the present rate it will become largest within a few years [2].

In spite of these achievements China still faces some challenges which are economic and geostrategic in nature. In keeping with its history which has been mostly peaceful the Chinese leadership has tried to find peaceful solutions to the problems confronting it.

President Xi Jinping proposed the idea of One Belt and one Road. Some US critics of BRI immediately questioned the concept of 'one belt and one road' in a highly globalized world. The US critics overlooked the content and got bogged down in lexicon. In any case now the concept is generally packaged under a more concise term i.e Belt and Road Initiative (BRI).

The scope of BRI, like the ancient Silk Roads is limitless in the sense that it cannot be restricted to any one region of the world. The idea behind BRI is to create a network of infrastructure spread over three continents i.e Asia, Africa and Europe, bringing together more than seventy states. If this gigantic project comes through it will create a win-win situation for all. BRI is an interconnected system of trade routes and other dimensions, which can help developing states to break the cycle of poverty and, join the ranks of prosperous nations. The blue print of BRI which is still in the process of evolution brings out several features. Firstly, the scheme should not be viewed only as a network of trade routes.

During the first phase roads, bridges, railway lines, air ports, seaports and other means of communication will be developed. A network of oil and gas pipelines will be developed, along with ware houses and cold storage facilities for traders. Hotels, motels and restaurants will also be needed for the convenience of traders. Buses, trucks and petrol pumps at regular intervals on various highways will be required. Small scale shops, tea stalls and other similar ventures on the way could open opportunities for people of lesser means.

Another important feature is the industrialization phase. Industrial parks, Special economic zones and Free trade zones will be created during the second phase. These projects can be launched simultaneously but good infrastructure and energy supply, will be essential for the smooth running and success of these ventures. To take an example the need for steel, cement and other construction material will increase substantially. Besides creation of millions of jobs, technological upgradation, expansion of training and educational facilities will also take place.

A book written in 2018 by Bruno Macaes under the title *Belt and Road A Chinese World Order*, has suggested that the Eurasian supercontinent has emerged in recent times, after the end of Cold War. Most people would welcome the development as it would promote integration but not Macaes. According to him the emergence of the supercontinent has not been according to Western model, but rather the result of Chinese endeavours. He regards this to be a negative development, however, many scholars from Asia and Africa may not perceive this as a negative fallout of BRI. The integration of Eurasia is good news for millions of people particularly in Asia who can hope for a better life.

The BRI also has its critics. Some experts and politicians from rival Western states believe that the project is too ambitious, others think it has been launched in a hurry without much preparation. Some critics particularly in the US show a lot of concern about the 'debt trap'. The environmentalists worry about the negative impact on the environment. Some of these arguments appear to be logical but some are motivated by spirit of political competition and geostrategic rivalry.

The project is ambitious no doubt, but to assume that it has been launched without planning would be incorrect. Several nations are involved, they vary in expertise, pace of work, cultural norms and working habits. Working together will help these nations to learn from each other, in order to improve their performance. Some countries suffer from bureaucratic hurdles, others from lack of experience, however, these are not insurmountable barriers. Within a few months and in some cases a couple of years things are expected to get better.

As far as accumulation of debt is concerned, we have to analyze the data before BRI and after the launching of development schemes under BRI. Debt issue has been a source of serious concern for many years prior to the launching of BRI. In the absence of infrastructure many developing states were unable to grow economically but they also had perceptions of insecurity. Some of these states had to take loans from World Bank and IMF to meet day to day economic challenges. Developing states often also incurred debt from commercial banks in the West in order to buy weapons from Western countries.

These transactions have resulted in transfer of resources from poor states to the rich. This is perpetuating poverty in developing states. In this sense debt trap has been there for a long time. In order to avoid 'debt trap' governments in Asia and Africa should set clear priorities as to which projects are essential for their economic growth. Expensive projects are often undertaken by states for their symbolism. The projects get publicity at home and abroad but from development point of view their value might be less significant.

Another point to remember is that governments should negotiate well in order to protect their interests. As stated earlier governments should take loans only for economically viable projects. The plus side of Chinese involvement is that there are no conditionalities [3]. The repayment schedule offered by Chinese institutions is comparatively easier. It is upto BRI participants to determine the criterion for selection of projects. Chinese government expects member states of BRI to take the initiative according to their own needs and circumstances. With more experience BRI will be better able to avoid pitfalls like Hambantota, which was the result of political and economic miscalculations due to inexperience.

In a report published by Xinhua on 9th January 2023 some relevant facts and figures have been presented. In the case of Sri Lanka according to its Department of External Resources (2021) a staggering 81% of the country's foreign debt was owned by US, European financial institutions, Japan and India. Of this debt China owns only 10% which clearly indicates that what Sri Lanka owes to China in terms of debt is a tiny fraction of the total amount. This debunks the China 'debt trap' narrative launched by the US.

As far as environmental issues are concerned all BRI projects are evaluated in terms of the projects impact on environment and no exceptions are made [4]. It needs to be added though that all governments try to keep a balance between need for economic development and protection of environment. Prosperity of people cannot be compromised and jobs have to be created, but at the same time environment has to be protected to avoid health problems and natural disasters. Opting for one at the expense of the other is not considered to be prudent policy. The policies I have analyzed so far appear to adhere to middle course, at times there might be a tilt in favour of one side or another, but this is an exception rather than a rule [5].

China has adopted serious approach vis-a-vis BRI, which can be gauged from the fact that at the start of the project, more than one trillion dollars have been allocated for building roads, railway tracks, oil and gas pipelines in addition to air ports and sea ports. Institutions have been established to promote BRI projects of which two deserve special mention:

The Asian Infrastructure Investment Bank (AIIB) has been designed to serve as a development bank for promoting infrastructure projects [6]. The bank was formed on 29 June 2015. In the same year according to a Chinese statement project worth USD 160 bn dollars were under various stages of construction. Some projects were also in planning state [7].

AIIB is promoting infrastructure projects across Asia and Africa. There is acute need for development of infrastructure in these two regions as these two continents lack modern infrastructure. There is a growing realization that there can be no economic progress without proper infrastructure. There is also an expectation that the whole process would lead Asian and African nations towards mutual cooperation and integration. Public will gain access to better social services. The Board of Governors of AIIB is a powerful decision-making body. The authorized capital of AIIB is USD 100 bn. China will hold 26% of voting rights.

The Silk Road Fund (SRF) was announced in November 2014. It is also a development fund of USD 40 bn. Its primary role is to provide funds for promoting various businesses as well as to invest in development projects. SRF provided funds for the Karot Hydropower project in Pakistan which is first project undertaken by SRF. The project is located fifty km from Islamabad [8]. The Chinese government has made commitment to provide 350 million dollars by 2022 to complete the hydelproject.

Another major step is the creation of linkages between different Universities with Xian Jiaotong University being at the centre of this alliance. The purpose of the alliance is to provide research and technical support for BRI. Academic collaboration for promotion of technological knowledge is another major objective. It will upgrade skills of young people in developing states. The linkages will not remain restricted to any particular field. Linkage between law schools will also be promoted in order to provide legal support for BRI related projects [9].

Silk Road Economic Belt i.e the land part of BRI was initially expected to have six tracks. One track had to be modified after India refused to join BRI. All tracks are making progress to varying degrees.

China-Mongolia-Russia Economic Corridor (CMREC) is a well-managed and rather smoothly running project. Mongolia lies between China and Russia, it also has common borders with Kazakhstan. Being land locked Mongolia is rather handicapped.

The relationship between the three neighbours had its ups and downs in the past, but generally it has been free of major conflicts. Mongolia has been trying to open up to the West now, whereas Russia and China have long established relations with the West, although they have not always been free of tension.

The state of infrastructure in Mongolia is in bad shape due to lack of foreign investment in this sector. The government of Mongolia was also unable to mobilize resources for the purpose.

In 2007 the government posted a new document 'The Millennium Development Goal based Comprehensive National Development Strategy of Mongolia'.[10] It set the goals of promoting economic development and creating viable energy projects. It also envisaged the development of infrastructure particularly railway and road networks. Since Mongolia is a major trading partner of China modernization of infrastructure is of prime value for both.

In 2001 'Millennium Road' project was floated to develop roads and railways but due to paucity of resources implementation of the project has been rather slow. Russia has been working with Mongolia on the project and tariff has not been increased since 2006 [11].

When China launched BRI one of the goals was to diversify trade routes, so that if one approach did not lead to promising results, it would not derail the entire process. China wanted to launch a route which would bring together Mongolia, Russia and China. The process has led to cooperation among the three neighbours, thereby, opening new avenues for the future. Gradually Mongolia is becoming a key transport corridor between China, Russia and Europe.

According to Professor Zhang Sujie 'there are three routes in the CMREC;' One is 1,963 Km long from Ulaanbaatar to the Port of Jianjin, the second route is 2,264 Km long from Choibalsan to the Port of Dalian, but the planned route from the eastern port of Mongolia Choibalsan to Jinzhou is 1,100 Km long which is the shortest route [12].

Mongolia being land-locked stands to benefit from the access given by China to use its ports. China's influence is also expected to grow in Mongolia. Since CMREC is not just a transit corridor but an economic corridor, it would give a boost to economic activity and cooperation, in the energy sector which is expected to be beneficial for all the three partners particularly Mongolia [13].

The hurdles in the case of CMREC are expected to be minimal, as there are no major disputes between the member countries. No regional or extra regional power is in a position to derail the project. The new routes would reduce distances and cut costs; they would therefore be preferable compared to old routes. However, according to Popova tensions did arise from time to time between the three neighbouring states. Mention has also been made of increase in tension between China and Mongolia. China and Kazakhstan have also faced tension over the issue of missing persons[14]. But due to absence of historical baggage and hopes of mutual gain through cooperation, the three participants have been better able to manage the problems.

China-Russia relations are becoming stronger since BRI was launched. Both countries hope to gain as a result of extension of BRI to Eurasian region. Russia launched the Eurasian Economic Union (EEU), in May 2015. China and Russia signed joint declaration on the integration of the SREB and EEU. The idea is to align the development strategies of the two groups in order to 'create a common economic space' [15].

After the integration of the two initiatives a lot of economic interaction is expected. Infrastructure development in the form of roads, bridges, oil and gas pipelines will strengthen trade ties and give impetus to connectivity, and cooperation leading to integration. The geoeconomic and geopolitical land scape of Eurasian region is in the process of transformation. If the process continues at the same pace regional states are bound to gain.

China, Central Asia and West Asia Economic Corridor or CCAWAEC is considered to be another promising venture [16]. It would give China easy access to Central Asian Republics (CARs) as well as to West Asian States (WAS). CARs and Middle Eastern States (MES) are rich in oil and gas. Pipelines could carry these much-needed resources to China. The pipelines in the Central Asian region are believed to be less vulnerable compared to the ones in the Middle East. During the last few years some parts of Middle East have been suffering from turmoil and political instability.

Syria has to some extent recovered from a devastating civil war fueled by many factors including the involvement of some regional and extra regional powers [17]. Yemen and Libya are still in the grip of conflict made worse due to involvement of some strong foreign powers. The devastation has been colossal raising concerns about the ability of these states to maintain their integrity and continued existence.

The US and European states are providing weapons to the rebels in Syria and Libya, even after promoting regime change in Libya. The US desire to promote regime change plunged them into civil war. The US failed in Syria but Libya is still suffering after the brutal murder of Libyan leader President Muammar Qadafi. Is all this being done deliberately to block the progress of BRI? Is this an effort to occupy sources of energy in order to create economic problems for China and other consumers? Another aspect could be the desire of arms manufacturing nations, to promote conflict in order to create further demand for their sophisticated weapon systems.

At a seminar attended by me in 2013 several scholars raised the point that wars add to poverty in developing countries while promoting prosperity in Western arms manufacturing nations [18]. Arms trade brings wealth and influence for Western nations particularly US. There is some truth in all of the above assertions. One can quote US government officials who openly admitted US involvement in these conflicts. In the case of Syria since natural resources are not a major factor, geostrategic context appears to be more significant. To help Israel by removing hindrances in the way of its expansionist approach and also to draw Iran into this conflict in order to weaken it [19].

Saudi-Iranian proxy wars had also benefitted the arms manufacturing nations, as Saudi Arabia and its allies are almost exclusively dependent on weapon supplies from Western countries. The Saudi-Iranian rivalry has been contained as a result of Chinese efforts. China helped the two to negotiate their differences. The success of China has established its credentials as a stabilising force. The situation is still fluid in the Persian Gulf with the threat of US launched armed conflict against Iran still on the cards. UAE-Israel normalisation of relations has further enhanced the threat, as the two are reportedly planning to convert UAE occupied Yemeni island of Socotra into a spying base. This will enable them to keep an eye on Iran, Pakistan and Chinese activities in the Indian Ocean with particular reference to Gwadar [20].

As long as the Middle Eastern states are unable to control the turmoil, CCAWAEC although potentially viable, would be unable to meet the high expectations attached to it. The idea that Israel could be a transit point, particularly after Chinese investment in expansion of Haifa is not workable. Israel is not a suitable transit point for Europe, because its aggressive policies can land it and the region, into a war like situation. As long as Palestinians are being persecuted and, illegal Jewish settlements are not dismantled, it would be morally and legally incorrect, to allow Israel to play any role in the project. Besides many regional states like Turkiye, Lebanon or even Syria as conditions there are moving towards normalcy, would be suitable candidates for the task.

CCAWAEC too is designed to be much more than a transportation corridor. An economic corridor requires peaceful environment, but this is a two-way relationship. The economic corridor when it comes into operation, it can strengthen peace and, promote economic development, industrialisation and creation of jobs[21]. It could also help regional states devastated by civil war to rebuild the infrastructure and to work towards the revival of their economies.

Another important Chinese venture in the Arab world is China-Arab States Cooperation Forum (CASCF) [22]. Its meeting was held in Beijing in July 2018. Representatives of twenty-two Arab states along with Secretary General of Arab League attended the meeting. Prior to that in 2014 sixth ministerial meeting of CASCF was attended by Chinese President.

The two sides have also signed MOUs on various subjects of mutual interest. China signed an agreement for production capacity cooperation with a group of Arab states. The SRF and AIIB have made investments in selected projects in several Arab states. According to IMF the Arab-China trade was up by 11.97% in 2017 to reach the figure of more than USD 195 bn. There is tremendous scope for further promotion of Arab-China relations in many fields.

According to President Xi Jinping China and Arab countries are natural partners in the Belt and Road Initiative. They are motivated by the best traditions of the Silk Road. For the last two thousand years there have been uninterrupted exchanges between the Chinese and Arab people. These exchanges were spread over land as well as the seas. China has recently upgraded its strategic relations with a number of Arab states. There has been cooperation in the field of energy, aviation and satellite technology.

CASCF is in addition to CCAWAEC. These are two separate ventures which bring China and different Arab states on one platform. Like CCAWAEC, CASCF also carries great scope for expansion in future since West Asia's geopolitical importance for BRI is indisputable. [23]

The hurdles which could slow down the progress of BRI in the Middle East were Iran-Saudi rivalry, but now it has been resolved by China. Internal instability in some states and US-Israeli nexus against other regional states remain as major hurdles. A conflictual environment can be exploited by antagonists who believe that progress of BRI will undermine their influence in the region.

The New Eurasia Land Bridge Economic Corridor (NEALBEC) is another ambitious project, its viability is beyond doubt. It links up East Asia with Central Asia and Europe. Another distinguishing feature is that this venture will link up the various corridors established under BRI. China has gained land access to Europe along with the maritime link. Infrastructure linking China with Europe is based on modern technology. The trains from China to Germany and other European destinations have reduced travel time by a big margin[24]. It is already in service and adds a totally new dimension to the Silk Road project. According to some experts it is a more expensive mode of transportation of goods, the maritime route would have been much more economical [25].

China-Pakistan Economic Corridor (CPEC) has been called the flagship project of BRI. It is also considered to be the most important track. A separate chapter dealing with CPEC is included in this volume; a detailed analysis of prospects for CPEC will be presented. It needs to be stated, however, that the project carries innumerable benefits for Pakistan and China. But due to hostile posture of adversaries the project also faces challenges.

China-India-Bangladesh-Myanmar Economic Corridor (CIBMEC) could have brought the four states together promoting cooperation between them. Some degree of pessimism surrounded the project from the beginning. India was critical when Bangladesh (BD) tried to benefit from China's offer of modernizing Chittagong Port. Since BD does not share a border with China and India has adopted a negative approach vis-à-vis China CIBMEC has not come through so far. China has, therefore, decided to adopt bilateral approach with BD and Myanmar.[26] China signed agreements to modernize sea ports in both countries.

China-Myanmar relations have shown good progress since the launching of BRI. It is also obvious that Myanmar is important for China's connectivity related projects. China-Myanmar relations were hindered due to guerrilla war going on near the Chinese border. China played a pivotal role in helping the Myanmar government and the rebels to settle their differences. The problem has now been resolved to the satisfaction of both parties and the route passing through the region, is playing an important role in the connectivity project.

Myanmar has at times suffered from political instability due to tribal hostilities, persecution of Rohingyas and other minorities and lack of trust in Civil-Military relations. This situation has historically provided big powers the opportunity to interfere in the internal politics of the country. According to Kaplan Western missionaries and some NGOs gained influence over separatist tribal leaders. The influence gained by these elements was an asset for the West when they were engaged in war in the region between 1939 and 1945.

Kaplan in his tour of Myanmar between 2008 and 2009 met some US citizens who had good knowledge of domestic politics of key regional states lying on the route of BRI. They offered assistance to US government in gathering intelligence, for the benefit of Western nations, against their adversaries. This could be done under the garb of missionary work, NGOs or any other suitable cover. Kaplan did not mention the individuals by their names, pseudonames like white monkey have been used instead[27].

If the US, Uk and other countries aligned with the West decide to take up this offer it will have the advantage of 'deniability'. Governments cannot easily deny their involvement if one of their officials is found involved in espionage or terrorism related crimes. But indirect involvement can lead to deniability. This aspect should be seriously considered by those who have been assigned the task of providing security to BRI.

Since Myanmar is regarded as a rather fragile state, opponents of BRI could use this frame-work in order to further destabilize Myanmar and other states associated with BRI. The goal could be to delay or disrupt the various tracks of BRI. The US could use this mechanism to impede China's access to Indian Ocean. Indians have been actively trying to prevent or disrupt China's direct access to Indian Ocean but they have not been successful so far. They could not dissuade BD and Myanmar from cooperating with China.

China and Nepal have signed several agreements aiming to promote cooperation at various levels. Nepal being land locked had to depend on India for transit facilities. Dependence on India made Nepal vulnerable to Indian pressure tactics. Nepal stands to gain from a system of international cooperation and access to transit facilities. China could provide Nepal with that access through other friendly states thus reducing its dependence on India.

China-Indochina Economic Corridor (CICEC) is designed to link the economies of East Asian states with that of China. Many ASEAN states are interested in improving trade and economic ties with China. They also expect to gain from infrastructure development schemes launched under BRI. Another expectation is, that improvement in infrastructure, will give impetus to further industrialization, leading to increase in volume of trade [28].

China has been interacting with member countries of ASEAN on bilateral and multilateral levels on regular basis. It happens to be a major trading partner of the economic grouping, the linkages nurtured over several years are beneficial for all the states involved in this exercise. At the same time, we have to keep in mind, that the tense situation in South China Sea (SCS), can be manipulated by powers who wish to scuttle CICEC.

China has undertaken diplomatic initiatives in the region which could go a long way in easing tensions in the region. It is expected that inspite of opposition CICEC could grow into a strong track of BRI. There are two major reasons for this optimism; firstly, China has not pursued aggressive policy against its neighbours in the past. ASEAN has taught regional states that cooperation is mutually beneficial. ASEAN states normally follow positive approach when they see prospects of gain through cooperation. The members of ASEAN are looking forward to Chinese assistance for further improvement of infrastructure and better connectivity between East Asia, Southeast Asia and other regions. Secondly, the reservoir of soft power and good will enjoyed by China is still largely intact and could play a significant role in paving the way for regional cooperation.

US Response to BRI [29]

President Xi Jinping has labeled BRI as 'Community of common destiny'. This concept was actually implemented by the Chinese leadership in their country. Development of infrastructure and reforms in every sector created what is known as the Chinese miracle. China's impressive achievements ensured the success of Chinese model of development. China has surplus economic resources which it plans to invest in developing as well as developed states in order to promote connectivity and cooperation.

Although infrastructure development leads to prosperity but it requires a lot of resources and takes time to show results. Perhaps because of this reason US and other Western nations donot have building of infrastructure in developing states as their top priority. Their main focus after World War II, was on containment of Communist states particularly Soviet Union. Building military bases in Asia, Africa and Middle East was considered more important, while building roads and bridges was under taken only if it was deemed to be necessary from military point of view.

As stated earlier the US has tried to oppose BRI on two grounds. They have tried to target BRI by using the concept of 'debt trap'.[30] Debt trap appeared on the political horizon when IMF and World Bank started trapping developing states in unbreakable shackles of debt. It created dependence to such a degree that these states had to take loans to pay previous loans. The BRI debt is expected to reduce dependence by making states stand on their own feet. The projects are expected to generate financial resources from which loans could be paid back.

The second source of criticism is the fear that China's influence is growing in third world countries. China's soft power is also growing [31]. If Chinese influence continues to grow at the current pace it will be at the expense of US. The US has actually lost some of its influence in Asia and Africa due to its frequent involvement in wars which it failed to win. The US policy of 'containment' of China has not yielded positive result.

After the Chinese government launched BRI the US adopted multi-dimensional strategy. At diplomatic level there is well orchestrated propaganda against BRI. Simultaneously, the US has launched its own infrastructure related projects. Attempts are also on to block China's way in Southeast Asia and other regions. Some of these attempts are political in nature, others carry military dimension which can at times be provocative. US actions in South China Sea (SCS) and East China Sea (ECS) carry the risk of military confrontation. The US has also tried to bolster its position by signing political alliances which also have clear military dimension. To prevent China from strengthening its political and strategic positions and, to discourage it from gaining leverage in world politics, the US has taken steps which will be focused on in chapter VII.

US considered Middle East to be important for several reasons. Its location is strategic and many maritime and land trade routes pass through it. Its population is quite large and the region produces considerable quantities of oil and gas. The US wanted to be in control of the region and for that reason, it has been involved in many regime change operations in the region. Their operations were successful in Iraq and Libya, where the leadership was believed to be pursuing policies not acceptable to the US. The US regime change operation failed in Iran and Syria. However, parts of Syrian territory with all the resources are still under US control.

Saudi Arabia-Iran rivalry served US interest firstly, by increasing Saudi dependance on the US. Secondly, it became easier for US to contain and isolate Iran. At a seminar to discuss the future of Silk Road held in shanghai several years back, some scholars were of the opinion, that if states inimical to BRI are unable to stop its progress, they might try other approaches. One of these could be promotion of turmoil in the region. The region is certainly going through a difficult phase and the US appears to have gained at least temporary respite. But whether it will be able to make long term gains from this situation is not clear.

One recent setback for US has been China's success in promoting reproachment between Iran and Saudi Arabia.[32] The long tug of war between the two Middle Eastern states ended. Diplomatic relations will be restored and normalisation of relations will take place. This development clearly reflects the emerging diplomatic clout and soft power of China. It will give impetus to the integration schemes already launched by China in the form of CCAWAEC and CASCF. Increase in the influence of China could further promote regional states interest in BRI.

The Western powers are apprehensive that BRI will challenge their economic supremacy in coming years. They desire to play pivotal role in formulating rules and regulations to control global trade. This is something the West would never want to sacrifice under any circumstances.

Successive US administrations have launched initiatives to revive US interests in the region. Obama administration came up with a number of initiatives to contain Chinese influence. The idea was to maintain US supremacy at all cost. Pivot to Asia[33] reflected a major shift in US approach. East Asia now seemed to be the main focus of US policy. Asia-Pacific Rebalance (APR) [34] was introduced as a policy to counter balance China and reinforce sagging US leadership.

The US administration also highlighted the role which India could play in APR strategy. Nisha Biswal the Assistant Secretary of State for South and Central Asian Affairs attended a seminar in 2014. She stated that now South and Southeast Asia can be 'integrated into one economic landscape'. This Indo-Pacific Economic Corridor (IPEC) is unique idea where US and Indian security, political and economic goals converge. It is based on US 'rebalance' towards Asia and India's 'look east' policy. [35]

This formulation clearly depicts the direction of future US policy in the region. Indian deep state also shares this percpective.[36] Although attempt has been made to present the scheme as an economic venture but the military dimension is also visible. Coordination of security and political dimensions in US-India equation is inherent in the scheme.

Obama administration launched APR mainly as an attempt to dilute the economic and political clout of China. Another objective was to promote coordination in military doctrine and strategy of member states. To put naval pressure on China it was thought necessary to build pressure in the Indian Ocean and South China Sea.

The Indian government knows that its hold over its Northeastern states is tenuous, there are several insurgencies going on in the region. India believes that the US military support to crush the liberation movements will be forthcoming, due to the strategic location and importance of these territories for the success of APR [37].

Donald Trump throughout his presidential campaign appeared to be critical of APR. One reason behind his opposition was probably his desire to do away with Obama's legacy. The project could also be opposed on grounds of ambiguity. The policy had both economic as well as military dimensions but it was not clear which of the two was the core objective. On the one hand it was designed to block Chinese influence in South and Southeast Asia, but on the other hand the idea of China-US cooperation seemed to be inherent in the scheme. Some regional powers feared that it could be the beginning of a China-US condominium [38].

After the election of Trump as president he floated a new scheme to contain Chinese influence. US Secretary of State Mike Pompeo made a speech at Indo-Pacific Business Forum on 30 July 2018, focusing on the idea of Indo-Pacific Economic Corridor (IPEC). A sum of 113 million US dollars was allocated for the project. The meager amount was clearly insufficient for the project it was supposed to finance. Energy and infrastructure projects were to be launched in South and Southeast Asia. Private sector was invited to play a pivotal role. IPEC is based on the idea that Indian Ocean and Pacific Ocean should be considered one economic and political zone [39].

'Indo Pacific' has drawn criticism from political and academic circles. The concept was developed by Trump administration; it was published by them before leaving office probably to put pressure on Biden administration not to abandon the scheme. There appears to be a fusion of neoconservative and neoliberal approaches designed to ignite a 'new Cold-War' directed against China. There are also a number of contradictions inherent in the scheme. The US quest for maintaining its dominant position could add to tension with China [40].

Indo-Pacific region starts at western coast of India and ends at the Pacific coast of US. According to Jackson the concept can be traced back to Kaplan's Monsoon. However, instead of starting debate on the issue it has rather stifled discussion[41]. On the whole US Indo-Pacific strategy dealing with a region which is too vast and diverse can lead to confusion.

The US role has to be highlighted with emphasis on three critical areas i.e military planning, foreign policy and economic and trade policies. The concept inherent in IPEC scheme is to expand the role played by US and to prolong its leadership in the region [42].

As already pointed out IPEC is multi-dimensional, based on the realization that the US could and should exploit rifts between regional states particularly in SCS. US involvement has encouraged countries like India to intrude into regional disputes in support of US further vitiating the political environment.

Trans-Pacific Partnership[43] initially came into being under US patronage but President Trump decided to withdraw from it as it was deemed to be harmful to long-term US economic interest. On 8 March 2018 it assumed a new name Comprehensive Progressive Agreement for Trans-Pacific Partnership (CPTPP)[44] It has the same eleven members who held membership of TPP; the member states are from Latin America, East Asia and Southeast Asia. Also known as TPP-II it is expected to play an important role in future.

The differences between TPP and CPTPP are comparatively minor. Some states have been given concessions on a few issues. There has been some modification of clauses dealing with Intellectual

Property Rights. CPTPP was supposed to be a pro-US grouping but nine of the eleven members have Free Trade Agreements with China. China applied for membership of CPTPP even at a time of military provocation by US. This has sent a positive message of Chinese intentions to developing states in the region. There are a few problems which need to be resolved.

Taiwan is also an applicant but a vast majority of states in the world regard Taiwan to be a part of China. The US is not favorably disposed to the idea of China's admission to CPTPP. Another issue is that if the US pushes Taiwan's admission to CPTPP, then China-US relationship would be further aggravated. Since decision is made by consensus if Taiwan is allowed to join as a member it will block China's admission to CPTPP.

No discussion of US antagonism towards China would be complete without discussing the role of Quadrilateral Security Dialogue or Quad [45]. US, Japan, Australia and India are members of the group. It started in December 2004 at the time of Tsunami. The four nations worked together to provide relief during the natural disaster. It was not envisaged as a permanent organization. There was little desire on the part of Australia for example to get involved in a grouping against China. In 2007 Quad decided to hold a naval exercise, the move was criticized by many states due to apprehensions that it will divide regional states, promote tension and shift focus away from economic cooperation.

It is now regarded as a full-fledged strategic grouping, some regard it to be an informal strategic forum. US proclaims its major goals to be establishment of a rule based global order[46], freedom of navigation, liberal trade system and mechanism for alternate debt financing[47]. China and many states have their doubts about the stated goals. The most important features of Quad appear to be military in nature. Naval exercises are a regular feature of Quad. Member states have been coordinating their naval policy in SCS, ECS and Indian Ocean.

The future of Quad is being debated in political and academic circles[48]. Its success depends on several factors; all the member states would make decisions regarding their future role in Quad, based on their long term national goals and objectives. Another consideration would be whether they see alignment of policy between the four to continue in future[49]. The nature of their bilateral relations with the US would also be factored in, but perhaps the most important consideration would be the level of perceived threat from China. US past performance and the degree of seriousness attached by US to Quad would also determine the future of Quad.

Some non-member countries have from time to time participated in Quad activities. The UK naval contingent recently participated in Quad naval exercise. However, attempts to lure other nations like Singapore, South Korea, Taiwan and some others to form Quad plus have not succeeded so far. UK has not formally joined Quad yet, but even if it does, it may not drastically alter the scenario in favour of Quad.

The formation of Australia-UK-US (AUKUS) [50] trilateral agreement is an important new factor. It came into being on 15 September 2021, UK and US have decided to strengthen Australian navy by providing it with nuclear powered submarines. This deal also includes transfer of technology along with the submarines. France is unhappy because Australia scrapped a deal signed earlier with it. France's relations with all the three countries have been adversely affected.

With this development a crack has appeared in the Western camp; the English-speaking nations are coming closer together, at the cost of relations with non-English speaking nations in Europe. This development was followed by attempts to control the damage. These efforts have been partially successful, the ambassadors who had been called back by France are back in Washington DC and Canberra. It is relatively easy to deal with outward signs of damage, but it is internal damage which is more difficult to fix.

In politics perceptions are often as important as reality. There are many examples to be found in history which bring out this fact. When nations decide which course of action to adopt the following factors might play a crucial role:

- National interest determines what policy will be adopted by a state[51]. There are only a few examples where a state seemed to deviate from its perceived national interest. National interest however, is defined by the political elite and a change in leadership can introduce a new interpretation of national interest.

- US has in the past on many occasions abruptly deviated from its stated policy due to a number of factors. President Obama launched a few initiatives which were abandoned by President Trump[52]. The ones launched by the latter also lost momentum due to paucity of funds and perceived lack of seriousness.

- Bipartisan policy measures and firm support of Congress would stand a better chance but they are rare. On some occasions US approach appears to be ambiguous to say the least.

- In my interviews with young and old alike the dominant feature was perception that US approach was negative, designed to retard China's emergence as a great power.

- Another drawback in US approach is fighting economic challenge posed by China (according to US perception) with military means. The response should be designed keeping the challenge in mind.

A response tilting in favour of military approach is not likely to lead to desired results.

Considering the above arguments it seems that the chances of success of BRI are brighter compared to IPEC. When states particularly developing ones determine their approach whether to join BRI or IPEC, all the above noted considerations will weigh heavily and might finally, be instrumental in shaping the outcome.

If BRI develops on lines which have been prescribed for it and, member states are able to overcome the challenges in their way, it will grow into the most ambitious project of the twenty first Century.

Chapter II

1   SREB is being researched and widely debated all over the world. The think tanks and universities in the West are also engaged in research on the subject. At times the criticism is politically motivated but some scholarly works also appear from time to time. Jeffrey Reeves 'China's Silk Road Economic Belt Initiative: Network and Influence Formation in Central Asia;' Journal of Contemporary China Published online 19 February 2018. https://doi.org /10.1080/10670564.2018.1433480

2   Its growth in first quarter of 2021 was a little over 18% but there was a sharp decline in the second quarter. According to Centre for Economic and Business Research (CEBR) it is expected to overtake US by 2028. http://bbc.com>news.

3   Conditionalities imposed by Bretton Wood institutions aggravate economic problems, thereby perpetuating dependency and need for more loans to pay the old ones.

4   Interview with Dr Shazia Ghani who deals with CPEC section in PM Secretariat mentioned that evaluation of impact on environment is an essential requirement for all projects.

5   http://www.researchgate.net

6   N. Litchtenstein 'Governance of Asian Infrastructure Investment Bank in Comparative Contex't http:// www.aiib.org.

7   Details of AIIB role in BRI's projects 'Zia Sarhadi, 'One Belt One Road Initiative' Crescent vol 46, no 4 June 2017.

8   720 MW project on River Jhelum https://nation. com.pk

9   Interviews with faculty from some of these institutions highlighted the main goals of this

exercise. The process is only at initial stage at present. Some faculty members pointed out some short comings as well.

10 Ekaterina Popova, Role of Economic Corridor: China-Mongolia-Russia in the Frame of Belt and Road Initiative, Budapest 2018 P 20.

11 Ibid

12 Ibid p 21.

13 However Mr Shepovalenko a Russian scholar was not entirely happy with the the pace of development of CMREC. He felt that member countries should provide further momentum to the initiative.

14 Popova, opcit P 28.

15 Serafettin Yilmaz, Yuo shifan, Liu Changming, 'Remaking Eurasia: The Belt and Road Initiative and China-Russia Strategic Partnership', Asia-Europe Journal, 22 May 2019 http://doi.org|10.1007|s10308-019-00547-1.

16 Gulf News 8 July 2018, Report of Eighth Ministerial meeting of the Cooperation Forum 'Focus on BRI'

17 In several interviews Hilary Clinton openly admitted the role of US in fomenting trouble in Syria and Libya to promote regime change in the two countries. At least one US president is on record having supported regime change in Syria and Libya.

18 President Eisenhower in his farewell address on 17 January 1961, raised the issue of US Military-Industrial Complex. http://www.eisenhowerlibrary.gov.

19 Hilary Clinton and General Ramsey Clarke gave interviews which revealed US plans to destroy six Arab and Muslim states in a period of five years starting in 2010.

20 The island is currently under the control of UAE. According to Ambassador Hasan Javed it is no

longer possible for states to occupy territory belonging to another state. He stated that UAE will have to return Socotra to Yemen after restoration of peace.

21 Arab world has a large pool of young population. Creation of jobs is important for political stability of Arab states. One factor behind 'Arab Spring' was lack of economic opportunities for Arab youth. The movement started in Tunisia.

22 Nino Jose Heredia, 'China and Arab States drew up a blueprint for cooperation in the new era', Gulf News 9 July 2018

23 Mehmood-ul-Hassan Khan, 'BRI: Engine of Growth,' *Defence Journal,* January 2018. p 32 www.defensejournal.com

24 It is true that normally maritime routes are cheaper but according to Frankopan the modern trains introduced by China are much faster than anything seen in the past. Peter Frankopan, *The Silk Roads A New History of the World* (Bloomsbury Oxford 2015) p 516.

25 Bokuan Chen, 'The Belt and Road Initiative: How European Businesses can Benefit', China Briefing 2 April 2018 www.china-briefing.com/

26 According to a report published in The Hindu the Chinese have dropped CIBMEC and in its place CMEC and Nepal-China Tran's Himalayan Multidimensional Connectivity (NCTHMC) have been mentioned. www.thhindu.com BD-China-India-Myanmar by M.A Karim 2018 has mentioned connectivity from China-Myanmar to Bangladesh by passing India http://pubs./c/arm.net

27 Robert D. Kaplan, *Monsoon The Indian Ocean and the future of American Power*, (Random House N.Y 2010) pp 223-224.

28 Pisinee Leelafaungsilp, 'China Belt and Road

Initiative: ASEAN perspective', CEIC Research Analyst http://info.ceicdata.com>China-bel

29 US is believed to be a power in decline, however some scholars believe that inspite of relative decline US will continue to be a dominant factor in world politics. Joshua R. Itzkowitz Shifrinson's 'Rising Titans Falling Giants' suggests that the policies of the two powers depend on a number of factors, but according to him rising power has more interest in promoting decline of the falling power, which is not clearly reflected in this case.

30 Chatham House 'Debunking the Myth of 'Debt-trap Diplomacy' 19 August 2020.

31 China's soft power is rising and is believed by some scholars to be a primary factor in promoting BRI. Mingjiang Li, 'Soft Power China's Emerging Strategy in International Politics' Lexington Boolis 2010 P 165, pp 170 – 171. Also see Syed Hasan Javed, 'Chinese Soft Power Code,' Paramount Books, Karachi 2014. pp 36- 37

32 Dawn, 11th March 2023

33 Kenneth G. Lieberthal 'The American Pivot to Asia', Brookings 21 December 2011, Obama did not refer to the term 'pivot' during his tour of Asia. Clinton mostly referred to 'pivot' in her statements.

34 For details see David J Bertearl, Michael J. Green and Zack Cooper, 'Assessing the Asia Pacific Rebalance,' CSIS December, 2014.

35 Nisha Biswal's remarks at University of World Economy and Diplomacy 2 December, 2014 https://2009-2017.

36 The 'rebalance' has a clear military dimension which has been stated in CSIS study referred to earlier p 5.

37 Uma Purushothamon and Nandan Unnikrishnan, 'A Tale of Many Roads: Indian Approach to

Connectivity Projects in Eurasia,' *India Quarterly* 18 January 2019, p4. India wants connectivity only under its leadership, excluding China. India's vulnerability in its Northeastern states is obvious in strategic sector but authors have highlighted economic and political dimension.

38　Ibid p.16 At a seminar some East Asian scholars were of the view that perhaps it was a deliberate move to create misgivings about future role of China.

39　Shankari Sundararaman; 'Indo-Pacific Economic Corridor' this article was originally published in GP-ORFs' Emerging Trans-Regional Corridors: South and Southeast Asia.

40　Lyle J. Goldstein 'Indo-Pacific Strategy is a Recipe for Disaster;' LAWFARE, 18 February 2021

41　Van Jackson, 'America's' Indo-Pacific Folly' Foreign Affairs 12 March 2021.

42　Sundararaman, opcit.

43　James Mc Bride, Andrew Chatsky and Anshu Siripurapu 'What's next for the Trans-Pacific Partnership (TPP)?' Council on Foreign Relations 20 September 2021

44　Ibid

45　Ambassador G.R Baluch 'The Quad Chariot and the new great game in Indo-Pacific' e paper 24 July 2021.

46　China regards US 'rules based international order' to be another smoke screen to promote US domination. Global Times 26 July 2021. http://epaper.globaltimes.cn

47　For details see The Quadrilateral Security Policy Dialogue: Towards an Indo-Pacific order HDP Envalt, Raja Ratnam School of International Studies, Nanyng Technical University, Singapore.

48　Ibid P 4

49 Ibid

50 http://economictimes.com>news.

51 Dr Luigi (Italian scholar) stated in his interview that states pursue their national interests at all costs. History suggests the same.

52 Jim Richardson, 'To Win Friends and Influence People, America Should Learn from the CCP.' Richardson served as director Office of Foreign Assistance at the US State Department.

CHAPTER III

China – Pakistan Economic Corridor: Connectivity and Cooperation

China – Pakistan Economic Corridor also known by its acronym CPEC is considered to be the flagship project of BRI. It is a project born out of years of cooperation between China and Pakistan. The two neighbouring states focused their attention on benefitting from opportunities that came their way. Over the years the two nations developed mutual trust which is an important component of all relationships including interstate relations. Another principle they adhered to was non-interference in each other's internal affairs. Pakistan learnt many lessons while interacting with the US during the Cold War and even after it ended. Its relationship with China has been shaped by lessons learnt by Pakistan during Pakistan-US relations.

A study of Pakistan-US relations since 1947 would bring out some important aspects, which should always be kept under consideration, by those who are responsible for formulating Pakistan's foreign policy.

The perceived commonality of interests between the so-called allies was short lived. The two countries had little in common, however, they came together because US wanted to use Pakistan and other developing states particularly if they held strategic value in the context of Cold War [1].

Idea which emerged from the US was to form a block of developing states, under the leadership of US as a bulwark against Communist states and their ideology. Most developing states including Pakistan had no problem with Communist States. Pakistan's main source of threat came from India, the newly established country needed to develop its military capability against the only threat to its existence. In order to develop its military capability Pakistan tilted towards the Western camp. Soviet Union was antagonised and after that fully supported India in all its conflicts with Pakistan.

For Pakistan it was a double loss. While India was fully supported by Soviet Union in the 1965 and 1971 wars against Pakistan, the US approach was ambivalent. US refrained from supporting Pakistan as it did not want to displease India.

When India conducted a nuclear test in 1974 instead of penalizing India, the US directed all its energies towards ensuring that Pakistan would not follow suit.[2] Many Pakistan specific sanctions were imposed which did great damage to Pakistan's economy.

In December 1979 Soviet forces entered Afghanistan, and the US took it as a challenge and decided to approach Pakistan. Pakistan also looked upon it as a threat in view of close Soviet-India relations. All the sanctions against Pakistan were removed. After Soviet withdrawal from Afghanistan (which could not have happened without the support of Pakistan and the courage of Afghan mujahideen) Pakistan's efforts were forgotten and the sanctions reimposed.

The next challenge came in the form of the so-called US war on terror. Many important questions arose for example was 9/11 an inside job? What were United States real objectives in launching the so-called war on terror? To cut a long story short the US once again approached Pakistan for support. In October 2001 (like the 1980s) the government in power in Pakistan, was not democratically elected and easily gave in to US pressure. Coercive diplomacy was used by the US against Pakistan. When the Musharraf government succumbed to US pressure tactics, Pakistan became battle ground between various armed groups. More than seventy thousand Pakistani civilians lost their lives, over five thousand military personnel also gave their lives.

Musharraf government handed over thousands of Pakistanis to the US [3]. Terrorism was launched against Pakistan some of which was sponsored by known adversaries of Pakistan. US occupied Afghanistan became a base for BLA, TTP and other terrorist groups operating against Pakistan. There was no economic development in Pakistan particularly from 2001 to 2013. The 'US aid' was no substitute for economic progress. The country suffered from the conditionalities imposed by IMF, there was a shortfall in production of electricity and the electricity produced was too expensive.

Under this scenario there was little hope for economic recovery and alleviation of poverty. However, the lessons learnt by Pakistan have shaped Pakistan-China relations. Major lessons for Pakistan are firstly, that unless there is mutual trust between the partners there can be no long lasting political relationship. Pakistanis are of the opinion that while Pakistan was cooperating with the US during the Cold War and 'War on terror' US was busy hobnobbing with India thus undermining Pakistan's economic and political interests [4]. On its part the US believes that Pakistan supported Afghan Taliban and was primarily responsible for US defeat at the hands of Taliban [5]. Another lesson learnt by Pakistan is that commonality of interests is necessary and no amount of coercive diplomacy can create it. If the interests of states do not converge then keeping the alliance alive would be an impossible task. Third most important requirement is mutual respect and non-interference in each other's internal affairs.

The world scenario has been undergoing major transformation particularly in the last two decades. Although US is still recognized as a major world power, but there is also a widely held belief that it's in decline. There is also confusion in Western ranks about various issues. After Brexit the UK-France dispute over fishing rights is ominous but even more serious dispute has emerged between US, Australia, UK and France on the issue of sale of submarines to Australia. US leadership of Western camp is eroding to say the least. On the other hand, the spectacular rise of China as an economic giant can hardly be denied. China has not fought a major war since the Korean war. China-India border skirmishes of 1962 and recent conflict in Ladakh, have been short military engagements resulting in Chinese victory. China's focus has now shifted to development of infrastructure and promotion of industrialization.

Chinese experience suggests that there can be no economic progress without modernisation of infrastructure. Keeping this lesson in mind China has come up with Belt and Road initiative (BRI), particularly its widely discussed CPEC project, is promoting connectivity and paving the way for cooperation. The focus of Pakistan's foreign policy has shifted towards geo-economics since 2013. Economic diplomacy is based on the realization that, in order to develop strong economic ties between nations proactive foreign policy is required. Perhaps there would have been no CPEC had there been lack of trust between China and Pakistan. CPEC would have been a pipe dream without the existence of Karakorum highway (KKH) which was constructed during the 1960s. For CPEC to succeed another vital link in the form of port facilities was required. This gap was filled when Gwadar became operational in April 2015.

CPEC Institutional Frame-Work Both partners have created a number of special institutions to facilitate decision making related to CPEC. These institutions are responsible for implementation of CPEC projects.

To expedite projects under CPEC a Task Force has been created which is headed in Pakistan by Minister for Planning and Development. The Chinese side is represented by Vice Chairman of National Development and Reform Commission (NDRC) The Task Force has morphed into the Joint Cooperation Committee (JCC) and is primarily responsible for implementation of CPEC projects. JCC basically regulates the working of subordinate Joint Working Groups (JWG). Decisions regarding whether to include a project under the frame-work of CPEC are made at the level of JWG and JCC only endorses those decisions. The approach followed here is bottom-up rather than top-down. There are ten working groups under JWG frame-work.

They deal with (i) Energy (ii) Transportation infrastructure (iii) Gwadar (iv) Industrial Cooperation (v) Security (vi) Policy Planning and Coordination (vii) Socioeconomic Development (viii) International Cooperation and Coordination (ix) Agriculture and (x) Science and Technology. These working groups are knowledge based and normally experts of relevant fields sit in JWGs.

Ministry of Transport leads the JWG dealing with Transport Infrastructure on the Chinese side. The Energy JWG is led by National Energy Administration (NEA). NDRC heads JWG on Gwadar and Industrial Cooperation and Planning. NDRC is supported by EXIM Bank, China Development Bank (CDB) and other financial and administrative bodies. Pakistan's Ministry of Planning, Development and Reform and China's International Development Cooperation Agency (CIDCA) Co-Chair JWG on socioeconomic Development. JWG on International Cooperation and Coordination is co-led by Ministries of Foreign Affairs of Pakistan and China [6].

CPEC Authority is an important institution dealing with issues related to CPEC. It maintains a website which is a major source of information. It also serves as a bridge between the two governments. The PM Secretariat also has a section dealing with matters related to CPEC.

Apart from this intricate network these institutions interact with preexisting ministries and departments in the two capitals. In Pakistan provincial governments also play their role. Coordination is of essence and any weakness in this area can have adverse impact on the projects. Even if it does not derail the process, it can be detrimental to smooth running of the projects.

CPEC has to go through phases each of which is designed to achieve clear goals and objectives. Advent of CPEC in 2013 created prospects for mutual gain for the two allies. The Early Harvest projects were designed to meet the challenges of infrastructure and energy shortage in Pakistan. Building new roads, railway lines and oil and gas pipelines were of immediate concern. Under this scheme a network of roads running from North to South and East to West were created. Railway lines were to be built inorder to connect various parts of Pakistan.

A number of oil / gas pipelines were also to be laid. Coal is a part of energy mix in Pakistan as it is locally available. Some coal fired power houses have already started functioning. Establishment of oil refineries was included in the Early Harvest phase. Power houses using all forms of energy including nuclear energy have been built. Thirty-two Early Harvest projects were completed within five years, 85000 jobs were created and these projects added between 1 to 2% to GDP. After that load shedding was reduced but the cost of electricity produced is still high. If this issue is not tackled soon goods produced in Pakistan will be more expensive compared to goods produced in other counties [7].

CPEC has been divided into three phases. In phase one the focus was on infrastructure and energy. These projects were to be completed on priority basis. First phase ended in 2018 [8].

The second phase has as its goal the promotion of industrial ventures like creation of Special Economic Zones (SEZ). Transfer of technology and creation of jobs will not only benefit the national economy, common people will also benefit. A number of social sector projects are also being launched.

Phase three will see the completion of Railways Mainline-1 and operationalization of all SEZs [9]. Phase three will be completed by 2030. Phases two and three together present the blue print of the 'Long Term Plan' of CPEC. A 'Long-Term Plan of China-Pakistan Economic Corridor' jointly produced by National Development and Reform Commission (NDRC), Peoples Republic of China and China Development Bank (CDB) came out in December 2015. It is the most elaborate blue print of the Long-Term Plan which I came across in November 2021. Spread over 229 pages it spells out in detail the future shape of CPEC.

The developments on ground do appear to follow this blue print, in-spite of the pandemic which engulfed the world for three years after the report was formulated. The construction of infrastructure is crucial for success of CPEC, as the two countries directly involved in the venture can interact with each other in various fields like trade, industry and tourism only if roads, railways and other means are available. Highway projects like Karakorum Highway phase II (Thakot-Islamabad), extension project of China's G 314, Lahore-Multan-Sukkur Highway extension project were all part of Long-Term vision of CPEC. The Early Harvest projects of infrastructure and energy were specially designed for Pakistan to meet the immediate problems. As and when the need arises infrastructure and other projects will be undertaken.

Railway network in Pakistan needs modernization and extension. Renovation and extension of ML-1, ML-2 and establishment of Havelian land port are part of Long-Term Plan. A railway project from Jacobabad to Gwadar is also included in the Long-Term Plan. In 2030 and beyond a new line from Kashgar to Havelian and, another passenger train between Karachi and Peshawar will be launched. Expansion and renovation of other railway lines is also on the planned.

Cooperation in the field of civil aviation has also been a major focus of CPEC. Building a modern airport in Gwadar, renovating and expanding Kashgar international airport, construction of Yarkant airport and Taxkorgan Pamir airport are part of the Long-Term Plan. Increasing the number of flights and establishing air routes connecting major Pakistani cities with those of China is also part of this scheme [10].

Gwadar port construction was also part of the Long-Term Vision [11], it was taken up on priority basis. Now it has become operational and is being provided with airport and other facilities.

Infrastructure of information network is another major undertaking under the frame-work of CPEC. China-Pakistan optical cable which is part of Long-Term vision will be 910 Km long starting from Tash kurgan all the way to Islamabad. It will result in creation of China-Pakistan optical cable and IT industry projects, strengthening the digital connection between the two partners. The idea behind China Pakistan cooperation in the IT sector is to develop a common information industry between the two neighbours.

A cross-border optical cable is also planned; it will start from Tash kurgan going along National Highway 314, it will reach Sust in Pakistan and finally reach Islamabad. Another major optical cable will connect Sukkur with Gwadar. For Medium and Long-Term phase a second route of major optical cable connecting Sukkur and Gwadar, will be laid upgrading the internet facilities in Pakistan. Digital television will be introduced all over Pakistan Covering 90% of the population. The technological upgradation will improve quality of broadcasts and performance of Pakistani media in general. An electronic surveillance system is also planned. It will cover border areas thus enhancing security of the two states.

Pakistan-China Cooperation in the Energy Sector

CPEC frame-work pertaining to energy covers all sectors, thermal and hydel power, tidal wave energy, wind energy, solar energy and nuclear energy.[12]

Nuclear power stations have already started functioning, more will be established in future. Solar energy parks are being established to help Pakistan benefit from this source available in abundance in the country. Tidal energy and wind energy can be made use of in coastal areas in particular. Pakistan has a long coastline of about 1050 Km, 800 Km of which is in Baluchistan and 250 Km in Sindh [13].

Thar Coal is also being used but NGOs dealing with environment often target these projects. Pakistan's Exclusive Economic Zone is expected to hold considerable oil and gas deposits but Western oil companies have failed so far in discovering these deposits. [14] Chinese oil companies should be given this project under CPEC, if they succeed both countries will benefit from this endeavor.

Although some energy projects were undertaken by China in Pakistan before CPEC came into being, but it was only after CPEC was launched that shortfall in Pakistan's energy production was considerably reduced. Additional 13,000 MW of energy were added to national grid in 2018. [15] Now the challenge is to reduce the cost of energy production. It was estimated some years back that Pakistan could produce 50,000 MW of hydroelectric power. The cost of production will be cheaper, but some local politicians on their own and often in collusion with India, have been opposing all dam construction projects [16]. These politicians have failed to come up with convincing arguments in favour of they stand so far. Federal government is restrained as it prefers to build consensus before taking practical steps on this issue.

Industrial Development Under CPEC

The main challenge for Pakistan is to speed up the process of industrialization in the twenty first century. Pakistan has a large segment of youth in its population. Jobs have to be created and skills imparted so that the country is able to benefit from CPEC. China is also planning to shift some of its industry to overseas locations. Pakistan is suitably placed to attract some of these industries. Under CPEC, Industrial Parks and Special Economic Zones, are being created in the core areas of CPEC.

There are two dimensions of this project; most of the industrial projects will be in close proximity to big cities, CPEC routes and other areas which have infrastructure and skillful younger population. However, there is also the need to avoid traffic Jams and congested cities. Areas in close proximity to cities but preferably not within them can be considered for this purpose. Another major issue is whether the Chinese will bring their own manpower, having relevant skills and experience, or employ people from the host country. The Chinese will probably opt for a combination of the two, some skilled and experienced people from China, working with majority of Pakistanis while helping them to learn new skills.

Transfer of technology to Pakistan is part of the Long-Term vision. China-Pakistan cooperation in the field of defense technology is flourishing, JF-17 Thunder aircrafts and Al-Khalid tanks already in use of Pakistan Air Force and army are shining examples of such cooperation. If anything, it would be easier for China to transfer industrial technology to Pakistan. Labour is cheaper in Pakistan, if other inputs like electricity are available at cheaper rate and uninterrupted supply can be maintained, then Pakistan would be able to develop its economy and break the cycle of poverty through its participation in CPEC.

In this context it might be helpful to establish industries based on natural resources available in the country. Zinc, Copper, rare earths, marble, graphite, pink salt and above all rare stones and gems can form a good base for Industrial development of Pakistan. [17]

CPEC panel has recently approved an ambitious plan to develop the coastline of Karachi. The Karachi Coastal Comprehensive Development Zone (KCCDZ) spread over 640 hectares (1,581 acres) on the western backwaters marsh land belonging to Karachi Port Trust (KPT) is a new scheme. The cost has been estimated at 3.5 bn dollars a 'direct Chinese investment'. The infrastructure in this zone will be comparable to the best in the world. Ministry of Maritime Affairs will be responsible for day-to-day management and coordination. There is no loan, it will be direct Chinese investment. It has kindled hopes of investments coming from all over the world [18].

The scheme appears to be extremely beneficial for the country but there are also a few problems. Half a million people (around 25000 families) will have to be relocated. Keeping in view past performance of governments, the slow pace of payment of compensation and the low rates of compensation, the people of the area are not eager to move out. The government cannot afford to alienate such a large number of people and yet the project is considered to be a 'game changer'. The government should device a mechanism which would satisfy the people and consolidate support not only for this project but for CPEC as a whole. It is worth remembering that such challenges are bound to arise in future also. But if a mutually satisfactory mechanism is developed now, it can be applied in future with relevant modifications depending on time and circumstances.

Agricultural Development and Food Security

Providing food security to a nation of 220 million people particularly in the presence of Indian machinations and lack of financial resources is a formidable challenge. [19] When CPEC was launched the planners tried to address this problem. It was decided that all along the route of CPEC agricultural, cattle and poultry farms will be established. Agriculture was to be the main priority and Chinese investment could have made the dream of agricultural self-sufficiency possible. However, it was not clear whether all this agricultural out put was to be exported to China or would be available for local market as well.

Pakistan's agriculture is faced with another major issue. Some western companies leading in the field of GM technology are Monsanto, Dupond, Syngenta and Bayer to name only a few. Since many Western countries have passed laws against GM food they are looking towards developing states for expanding their business. Pakistan has attracted their attention and the political parties in the National Assembly without realizing the implications of GM food for public health hurriedly passed the new Seed Bill [20]. Very few studies have been done regarding long term implications of this policy. Social scientists fear that small farmers might be wiped out leading to social unrest.

Under the Long-Term Vision prepared by NDRC and CDB the idea presented is to produce food and clothing for the general public at low cost. Agriculture will be mechanized and high scale of production ensured. Improvement in per unit yield of rice, wheat, cotton, and sugarcane was a key target of the plan. All these farms are to be promoted all along the corridor.

Development of product processing facilities in the rural areas and along the corridor is another major aspect of the plan. Food processing units like juice factories, ketchup producing units and establishment of fruit canning industry would lead to sound agrobased industrial base. Rural areas would gain tremendously as jobs would be created. Income generation avenues would appear thereby reducing poverty.

Promotion of storage facilities for farm products is also deemed to be necessary. Fish processing and storage facilities particularly in coastal areas could enhance the coastal economy. Other sea products like prawns and crabs would also require processing and storage.

There is provision in the Long-Term vision prepared by the Chinese, for cooperation and coordination in the field of agricultural research and development between China and Pakistan. Plant and animal diseases specially if they take the form of an epidemic can devastate rural economy. Research Organizations need to be created with mutual cooperation to face future challenges [21].

Promoting Water Supply and storage Facilities

Water plays an important role in ensuring human health and survival. One major problem faced by Pakistan and other developing counties is lake of clean drinking water. It is a major health hazard particularly for children. A lot of diseases like typhoid, various types of hepatitis, gastroenteritis, cholera etc are caused by unhygienic water. Underground water and even river and lake water is often found to be contaminated[22]. Sometimes pipelines carrying sewage water and fresh water run parallel to each other. If the sewage system and the fresh water pipeline are damaged for any reason, the fresh water gets contaminated.

Realizing the magnitude of this challenge NDRC-CDB Report presents a practical plan to deal with the problem. Water treatment facilities will have to be established / renovated. Water treatment plants do exist but their maintenance is poor, moreover they cater to a small segment of population. These facilities need to be expanded to cover both urban and rural population of Pakistan[23].

The drainage system needs to be reorganised and sewage water collection and treatment centres ought to be established. In many countries sewage water after treatment is made available for gardening which is considered safe for human health and environment. The sewage water allowed to flow into the seas and oceans should also be treated so that it does not harm marine life.

Pakistan will become a water scarce country in the near future if immediate steps are not taken now to redress the problem. China is helping Pakistan to build dams to store water. These projects are special targets of terrorists and apart from harming the projects Pakistan-China relationship is also being targeted. One aspect which is missing in the report, but is never the less, crucial to achieving water security is establishment of desalination plants. The scientists of China and Pakistan should also study the efficacy of drip agriculture and other water conservation strategies. Research and development need to be promoted in the field of water management.

Development of additional water resources can proceed along two lines; through the use of technology with China's assistance eg establishment of desalination plants. Treatment of sewage water (for gardening) could also provide relief. Building dams and storage of rain water and melted snow will be part of strategy one i.e application of technology for solving water problem. The second part of strategy should be political in nature. India cannot be permitted to pursue its policy of 'water terrorism' against Pakistan. It should not be allowed to deprive Pakistan of its rightful share of water. A political strategy will have to be devised to convince India that its present policy is unacceptable. There should be a clear time frame attached to negotiations. When it comes to flow of rivers India is in a weak position vis-a-vis China. The support of China could play a crucial role in Pakistan-India negotiations on the water issue. According to International Law too India is on weak grounds, as it cannot unilaterally abandon an international treaty without consequences.

The water issue is extremely important for peace between provinces and also for agricultural and industrial development of the country. The planners and decision makers should look ahead at least twenty-five years, to determine the scope of future challenges. The population will increase and so will the need for water.

Promotion of Tourism Under CPEC

Pakistanis are known for their hospitality and they take great pride in keeping alive this tradition. In the Long-Term Plan (LTP) tourism occupies a prominent place. In the first phase of LTP coastal belts of Sindh and Baluchistan have been focused on by the two sides [24]. Development of hospitality industry in the form of good quality restaurants, and hotels serving sea food will be appreciated by tourists. The promotion of yachting, boating, surfing and other water sports would also be popular. The development of discos, casinos, and other similar projects may be viewed with misgivings by some sections of Pakistani population. These steps might be necessary from the perspective of promoting tourism, but on the other hand, there is a risk of losing public support for the project. Such dichotomies are not uncommon in developmental programmes, but solutions have to be designed keeping public sensitivities and government priorities in view.

Pakistan has some of the world's highest peaks, from the perspective of scenic beauty they stand out. A number of tourists interested in mountaineering visit Pakistan every year, however, more can be done in this area. Among other scenic places there are waterfalls, lakes and woods which can be made more attractive by establishing good motels, restaurants and sporting facilities. Skiing is popular in Northern areas of Pakistan, Polo is another popular game which has been going on for many centuries. Tourists from all over the world visit to watch the game played by local teams. It can be institutionalized and teams from other countries can be invited to participate in the yearly event.

Among places of historical value Taxila, Harappa and Mohenjo-daro stand out. Taxila had the first university established in this region at least fifteen hundred years ago. There are relics of Buddhist and Sikh eras. There are many religious sites and Pakistan can benefit from religious tourism. Having a rich past Pakistan is ideally placed to attract tourists, who have interest in history or are motivated by natural beauty of land.

I met a tourist who visited KKH which is often considered to be one of the wonders of the world. She spoke highly of natural beauty around KKH and Attabad Lake, but what impressed her most was a glimpse of the ancient Silk Road, which runs parallel to KKH for many miles.

Guided tours for foreign tourists would be appreciated, this could provide a good learning experience for those who have interest in culture and history. There is a good aquarium in Karachi but a Professor of Biological Sciences from a foreign university suggested that more such centres need to be developed. They add to knowledge while also providing recreation. Pakistan has wide variety of aquatic life which can attract specialists from within the country and abroad.

From the cultural point of view as well, Pakistan's heritage is rich. All the provinces have a variety of cultural traits like folk dances and folk music. Story telling was a special feature of cities around the Silk Road. Kisakhani Bazar in Khyber Pakhtun Khwa (KPK) province of Pakistan has kept this tradition alive even in this age and era. Modern centres having tradional setting can be developed where professional story tellers tell old tales in local and foreign languages. Story telling competitions can be held with participation of tourists.

Local dances like Bhangra, Khattak, Luddi, Jhumar, Do-Chapi, Hareep, Dumhal and Lakri are famous dances from the provinces of Pakistan. Similarly all the provinces have their folk music which sounds heavenly. The food has certain similarities but also variations. Pakistan has so far not devised a strategy to benefit from this cultural diversity. Variety shows depicting dominant aspects of provincial dances and music can be arranged. Food streets can be established to offer wide variety of Pakistani cuisine. Foreign visitors relish Pakistani food[25].

Young people will have to be trained as tourist guides, story tellers, cooks, food servers, dancers, singers and hotel managers. Clean drinking water, gymnasiums, medical facilities and other infrastructure will also be required. All this needs financial investments. The Government of Pakistan along with Pakistani investors, can get good return for their investments if law and order is maintained at all cost. There is a lot of scope for tourism in Pakistan.

Knowledge Corridor

An important feature of CPEC is the plan to establish a number of knowledge corridors all through the routes of CPEC. The Knowledge corridors will be established in Gwadar and other cities serving as nerve centres of CPEC. There will be educational centres, vocational centres and institutes to impart various types of skills. Learning of Chinese language for Pakistanis and Urdu for Chinese citizens is being given due importance [26]. Research centres will also need to be established to provide input related to specific industries, agriculture, banking and managerial skills. Special Economic Zones (SEZs) will also receive guidance and research input from these knowledge corridors. The intellectual base would grow further as a result of this exercise and, culture of research will draw inspiration from the creation of knowledge corridors.

Mining and Natural Resource Development

Pakistan is rich in natural resources but the problem is, that little effort was made to establish industries based on these resources. There are studies suggesting that export of resources in raw form often leads to conflict and 'resource curse' particularly in the absence of strong institutions[27]. Many of CPEC mining projects will be in Baluchistan and Khyber Pakhtun Khwa (KPK) and some in Punjab and Sindh. For developing natural resources, the country needs technology, financial resources efficiency of work force and honesty of supervisory authorities, mostly bureaucracy in the case of developing counties. The agreements signed with Multinational Corporations (MNCs) normally specify the depth to which digging can be done and the amount to be extracted per year [28]. The companies sometimes flout these conditions and the bureaucrats and politicians who are supposed to keep a check on these activities simply turn a blind eye.

In some cases, due to lack of technological skills crude methods are applied due to which a lot of resources are wasted. The emerald mines in Sawat paid a heavy price when Pakistani Taliban occupied them. They lacked technological skills, thus they conducted blasts in the mines. As a result a lot of this resource was destroyed. The small amount obtained was smuggled to India to finance the war of terror against Pakistan. Promotion of technological skills should cover all stages from mining and extraction of resources to refining and manufacture.

In July 2015 the federal government proposed the establishment of twenty-nine Industrial Parks and twenty-one Mineral Zones. Certain areas in the four provinces were marked for the purpose. In Baluchistan province Khuzdar, Chaghi, Qilla Saifullah, Saindak, Reko Diq, Kalat and Lasbela were to have Mineral Economic Processing Zones (MEPZ). KPK was to have seven MEPZ. The areas mentioned were Dargai, North Waziristan, Kurram, Besham, Nizampur and Mohmand. In Punjab Salt Range and Chiniot and in Sindh Thar and Lakra were to get investment for establishing MEPZs.

Baluchistan Table I

Place	Natural Resources
Khuzdar	Chromite, Antimony
Chaghi	Chromite
Qilla Saifullah	Chromite, Antimony
Saindak	Gold, Silver, Rare earths.
Reko Diq	Gold, Copper, Rare earths.
Kalat	Iron One
Lasbela	Magnese

KPK Table II

Place	Natural Resource
Dargai	Chromite
N.Waziristan	Chromite
Kurram	Antimony
Besham & Nizampur	Iron Ore and lead
Mohmand	Marble
Waziristan	Copper
Chitral	Antimony

Punjab Table III

Place	Natural Resource
Salt Range	Antimony
Chiniot	Iron ore

Sindh Table IV

Place	Natural Resource
Thar	Coal
Lakra	Coal.

Data for all the tables is available at http://www.thenews.com.pk and http://cpec.gov.pk

Other natural resources are precious and semi-precious stones. There is considerable scope for establishing jewelry industry. Gas was found in abundance in Baluchistan during 1950s. Now these reserves have been depleted and gas shortages are becoming common particularly during winter. Exxon Mobil a US oil and gas company was given the task to prospect for oil and gas in Pakistan's Exclusive Economic Zone (EEZ). Initially they seemed optimistic but later came up with negative report. Many experts are of the opinion that the task should be given to a Chinese or Russian oil company. It would go in China's favour if oil is found so close to home and on the territory of a close ally.

Spatial Frame-Work of CPEC

CPEC is considered to be the most ambitious project of infrastructure development. It aims at promotion of peace and cooperation launched in the twenty first century. In practical terms it is much more than an infrastructure project. As stated earlier China's experience suggests that, there can be no economic and social progress without dependable and modern infrastructure binding nations together. Infrastructure development projects, therefore enjoy central place under CPEC.

At present China and Pakistan are the only members of CPEC but as the project is designed to promote regional cooperation the doors have been kept open for other regional states to join. CPEC plus can become a reality. Afghanistan and Central Asian Republics (CARs) being land locked states can gain several advantages by joing the regional cooperation frame-work.

At present CPEC begins in Kashgar a historical city in Xinjiang the Uyghur autonomous region of China. After crossing southern Xinjiang it passes through Khunjrab Pass entering the Gilgit-Baltistan region of Pakistan. It passes through KPK province to enter Baluchistan culminating at Gwadar. Karakoram Highway (KKH) serves as a backbone but the project became feasible due to Gwadar. KKH provides the shortest route from Kashgar to Gwadar, any other route would have been much longer. Many big and small cities in China and Pakistan all along CPEC route will also gain directly from the project.

In Pakistan there are three routes of CPEC; the Western route is the original and shortest route. It starts at Gwadar, passing through Turbat, Panjgur Khuzdar, Kalat and Quetta it enters KP continuing onwards to Abbottabad, Hassan Abdal then Islamabad DI Khan, Peshawar and Kohat it finally enters Gilgit-Baltistan and through Khunjrab Pass it enters China. It passes through hilly areas of Baluchistan and KP, the northward journey is also all hilly [29].

The Eastern route is more than 3000 Km being the longest route. It includes 1152 Km of Motorway linking Karachi with Lahore having 6 lanes and a speed of 120 Km/per hour [30]. Eastern route starts at Gwadar following the highway which runs parallel to Makran coast, the highway leads to Karachi and then on to Hyderabad, Sukkur and onwards to Punjab. Multan, Lahore, Islamabad are among the cities on the Eastern route. It leads to KP, major cities on the route being Abbottabad and Manserah. The eastern route then enters Azad Jammu and Kashmir (AJK) passing through G-B and Khunjrab pass it enters China.

The Central Route starting at Gwadar and passing through Panjgur, Khuzdar, Ratodero, Kashmore, Rajanpur, DG Khan it enters KP touching on cities like DI Khan, Hassan Abdal, Abbottabad, Kohat and Peshawar. All the three routes start from Gwadar and culminate in the north.

A Federal Minister who was given the task of implementing CPEC projects in an interview to Dawn on 15 May 2015, threw light on some important aspects. He stated the work on CPEC projects was supervised among other departments by joint working group. According to him some groups in the country were unnecessarily trying to politicize CPEC. Even before the joint working group had the chance to call a meeting regarding establishment of SEZs, IPs and FTZs some people started giving statements regarding future policy.

It was illogical and irresponsible according to him to do so.

Domestic Environment and Security Challenges for CPEC

The project could have been launched in 2014 but due to agitation in Islamabad the project was delayed till 2015. When some province is governed by a party which is not in power at the federal level this can lead to slowing down of projects. Party politics should not be a hurdle in the implementation of developmental projects and generally it is not. When it does happen it not only sends wrong message to other countries but also slows down the process and makes revival difficult[31]. Within provinces also the more influential politicians often attempt to divert the route and projects to their constituency inorder to reap electoral benefits.

Charges of diversion of routes may sometimes be used by some politicians for the purpose of point scoring against their political rivals. While doing so they ignore the consequences of their behavior in terms of message conveyed to people within the country and abroad [32]. Some politicians have deliberately tried to politicize developmental projects like CPEC[33] Another issue which is given a lot of importance by politicians concerns the question as to who should get credit for the project particularly if the project was launched by a political rival.

It has been noticed that sometimes agreements with MNCs and foreign powers are not negotiated properly. This could be due to lack of negotiating skills, ignorance or corruption. This is among the most crucial developments for a developing country. An MNC operating in Baluchistan which did not perform according to expectations was nevertheless awarded financial benefits by an international tribunal for several reasons, one of which was a poorly negotiated document having flaws to begin with. [34]

As pointed out in another section inadequate supervision by political governments and bureaucracy are also responsible for losses suffered by the country. It could be due to corruption or negligence. This has been happening in some other countries as well. The matter should be taken seriously and loopholes closed, so that developing states do not have to suffer at the hands of Western MNCs.

Another problem occurs when a new government takes control. The government takes time trying to understand the issues, the process might be prolonged.[35] The problem is compounded in case of lack of ownership of the project on the part of the new government. This happened in Pakistan in 2018 when a new government took charge in Islamabad. There are reports for example that ML-1 project was delayed because of some procedural issues involving China and Pakistan [36].

Planning and Development Minister on the other hand assured the nation that CPEC had not slowed down. In his press conference he rightly mentioned increase in instances of terrorism due to involvement of foreign powers inimical to CPEC[37].

Security is a major requirement for all developmental projects but if a foreign power is involved the matter assumes even greater significance. While the US was in occupation of Afghanistan, India used Afghan soil to conduct acts of terrorism against Pakistan. Another base which India built to promote terrorism in Pakistan was Chahbahar.

The US plunged into the Afghan war in October 2001 without making a serious effort to understand the situation. The US showed lack of understanding of Afghan history. It would not be wrong to say that Afghanistan throughout history has proved to be a graveyard of empires. British efforts to subdue the Afghans resulted in failure. Soviets invaded not for building an empire but to protect socialist revolution in that country, they were unsuccessful in their endeavor. The US failure to subdue Afghans was also due to a combination of geographical, historical and political factors. The change in Russian strategy too was not anticipated by the US [38].

Both Pakistan and US realize that their relationship is beyond repair. Under the new scenario both countries are looking for allies in order to fill the vacuum. Pakistan has had close relations with China for many decades but now this relationship has been further cemented. China's rise as an ascending economic and political power has intensified apprehensions in US and its allies. However, majority of developing states including Pakistan consider it to be highly beneficial for their future development.

Pak-China cooperation has taken many forms, it is based on shared interests. After acquiring access to Gwadar, China is no longer only a Pacific power. Direct access to Indian Ocean has made China a two Ocean power. This linkage has reduced the geographical distance between China, its markets and sources of raw material. China and Pakistan consider this to be a great economic asset which is mutually beneficial. However, US, India and some other countries look at this whole scenario in strategic context. Their perceptions suggest that the project will further enhance Chinese influence in the region. According to US perception any gain in Chinese influence will be at the expense of US. Many Western nations unfortunately view China's gain as their loss. If they remain attached to the zero-sum model and there is no change in their mindset, it could lead to more tension in their relationship with China.

The US and India have openly adopted negative approach towards CPEC and other BRI tracks. A two pronged approach has been adopted. At diplomatic level propaganda against CPEC and the entire concept of BRI has been intensified. The US also launched some infrastructure projects to divert attention away from BRI. The impression created about these US launched projects is that they were launched in panic without much preparation. It is probably due to this reason that developing states response so far has been rather cautious. A more serious aspect of the anti-CPEC strategy adopted by adversaries pertains to the use of terrorism. India was using Afghan territory under US occupation to scuttle CPEC. Terrorist organizations like Baluch Liberation Army (BLA) Baluch Liberation Front (BLF) Tehreek-Taliban Pakistan (TTP) and some others were generously funded by India. After US defeat and military withdrawal from Afghanistan India's anti-CPEC plans have received a setback [39].

After liberation of Afghanistan the future of CPEC is expected to become more secure due to two factors. When the Afghan government becomes stable it might show desire to join CPEC. If Afghanistan opts for CPEC then it will provide much needed link between Central Asian Republics and Pakistan. This could lead to further expansion of the corridor as landlocked states of Central Asia stand to gain from this connectivity project. Regional cooperation would benefit all the states including China. Chinese investment in

Afghan mining sector and infrastructure projects would create jobs and Special Economic Zones and other industrial ventures would lead to poverty alleviation. Many of the problems confronting Afghanistan might be resolved by joining CPEC.

India tried to bring Iran under its influence inorder to surround Pakistan from three sides. US which imposed economic sanctions against Iran nevertheless allowed India to build the Chahbahar port. This seems even more surprising if we remember that the US discouraged Pakistan from Joining Iran-Pakistan oil/gas pipeline. The project would have benefitted Pakistan. Iran completed the work on its side but Pakistan could not due to paucity of funds. India also established a terrorist network inside Pakistan using Chahbahar as a base.

The Iran-India nexus became weaker after India tried to befriend Arab states in the Persian Gulf. It is in the process of establishing strategic relations with UAE, Saudi Arabia and Bahrain. Will India be able to balance its relations with Iran and Arab states in the Persian Gulf? That may be easier said than done. The US calculation in letting India help Iran was to indirectly control Iran through India. It would also keep China out and prevent China-Iran relationship from developing into a formidable bond. Although India took the projects in Iran but perhaps under US pressure it adopted go slow approach. The pace of work was slow in Chahbahar and the connectivity projects, to connect Chahbahar with the northern border of Iran never took off the ground.

Iran has taken back this project from India and China might be invited to takeover the project. Another interesting point which emerged a few years back was Iranian expression of interest in joining CPEC [40]. On a number of occasions Iran has proposed linking Chahbahar with Gwadar [41]. If Gwadar and Chahbahar are to be linked together a few pre requisites will be required. There will have to be dependable infrastructure in the form of roads, bridges, railway lines and oil and gas pipelines linking the two ports. India's terrorist network and spying centres which they installed in Chahbahar will have to be dismantled.

What is Russian approach to CPEC? Few years back the media in Pakistan started discussing the idea of Russia joining CPEC as a full member but not much came of that idea. However, one very positive aspect of emerging political dynamics in the region is strong China-Russia relationship. Western scholars while discussing, China-Russia relations in the context of Central Asia treat the two as competitors. They hardly ever look at the cooperative aspects of this relationship. My chapter on BRI network in Central Asia briefly deals with the issue. Russia has shown interest in pipeline projects to be laid for supplying Middle Eastern oil and gas to China. A network of pipelines going in all directions particularly towards China will be needed in future.

Now that Afghanistan is free and not ready to allow its territory, to be used for terrorism against neighboring states India is in a desperate situation. 'Sleeper cells' of terrorists exist within the country and they might be responsible for the recent surge in terrorists activities. The problems mentioned above belong to a variety of categories therefore, each needs to be tackled differently. However, the good part is that they are not impossible to resolve. What is required is better coordination between different departments.

Accountability is necessary but it should not be politicized. If some laws have out lived their utility they can be replaced with better and more effective ones. Negotiations with foreign firms, need to be done more professionally and supervision of foreign firms, working on CPEC and non-CPEC projects should be more effective. Changing mindset is a more difficult issue and it is also time consuming, but progress will not be possible unless all political parties own the developmental projects. Effective intelligence both human and technological is a must. As far as strategy to eradicate terrorism is concerned, a combination of political and military aspects might offer a way out; winning minds and hearts can be tried successfully in many cases; it is a long-lasting solution but in the case of die-hard terrorists use of force becomes necessary.

CPEC in the Context of Regional Politics

International politics is in the process of transformation and the most visible indicator of change is realignment of states. India was a member of Non-aligned Movement (NAM) enjoying good relations with Soviet Union throughout the Cold War. It also signed 'Treaty of Friendship and Cooperation' with Soviet Union due to which the Soviets tilted towards India in the Pakistan-India war of 1971. India has moved closer to the US since the disintegration of Soviet Union. The signing of Civilian Nuclear Deal between US and India has aroused apprehensions in Pakistan. It is 'Civilian' in name but its military dimension is not hidden from anyone. India will now be able to divert more resources towards expansion of its nuclear arsenal. US plans to develop India as a counter weight to the rising power of China. Many strategists believe that it is beyond India's capability to counter China. However, India is being supported by US, it might use that power to bully its smaller neighbours in the region.

Pakistan on the other hand was known as the 'most allied ally' of the US throughout the Cold War years. Even during the 1960s and 70s US started taking Pakistan for granted. US gave no support to Pakistan during the 1965 and 1971 wars. It also did all it could to prevent Pakistan from developing cordial relationship with China. After India's nuclear test in 1974, US did not impose any sanctions on that state. It focused all its attention on preventing Pakistan from acquiring nuclear capability. There are several factors which have fueled tension between Pakistan and US in recent years. The US inability to achieve victory in Afghanistan further aggravated Pak-US relationship. Most senior US officials find it hard to accept the bitter reality of defeat at the hands of Taliban. They blame Pakistan for their failure.

In view of emerging Iran-China relations, oil and gas from Iran will be part of the mix. Due to China's policy of diversification, it will not depend on oil only from the Arab states of Persian Gulf.

The regional grouping CPEC seems to be gaining momentum. Even if new states do not join CPEC as members for now, a number of them would like to benefit from the opportunities provided by it. It might be a good idea for Pakistan and China to determine the frame-work under which new members might be admitted.

CPEC offers tremendous opportunities for China, Pakistan and regional states to cooperate for mutual benefit. Being part of BRI its success will pave the way for other BRI initiatives. For the success of CPEC it would be crucial to improve coordination between the member states. As stated earlier in future many states might want to join the regional grouping. Expansion would further enhance the importance of CPEC.

CPEC has aroused hopes of a better future among regional states but it is also true that adversaries are experiencing fear and dismay. The cause of their despair is the feeling that success of this initiative will spell the end of their political and economic domination. It is now quite apparent that political relationships in the region are being transformed. Under the new scenario smaller states stand a better chance to benefit from emerging opportunities. CPEC became possible due to decades of friendship based on trust between China and Pakistan. The "all weather friendship" will grow even more in future due to increasing economic interaction. The strategic changes taking place in the form of Chinese presence in the Indian Ocean, and Russian interest in the revival of regional trade routes, needs to be viewed in its proper context. The primacy of economic and trade relationships has opened up avenues of cooperation in other areas. Viewing world politics through the zero sum prism appears to be more costly and therefore less attractive.

Chapter III

1   The US gave this anti-Communist alliance a clear military dimension. This probably should have been expected coming from 'military-Industrial complex'. More about this in coming chapters

2   US Secretary of State Kissinger met Indian PM Indira Gandhi soon after the Indian nuclear test. He is reported to have said something to the effect that Indian nuclear test is fait accompli but how can US and India work together to contain the fallout meaning US-India cooperation in dissuading Pakistan from going nuclear.

3   Dr Aafia Siddiqui an MIT educated expert was handed over to US during Musharraf era. She is still in US prison on trumped up charges. Over five thousand other young people were also handed over to US.

4   According to public opinion survey conducted in 2019 in major cities of Pakistan, the majority of Pakistanis 65% did not consider US to be friend of Pakistan.

5   US seems to be looking for a scape goat to blame for its defeat. However, an objective and dispassionate study would pin-point a number of mistakes made by US strategists.

6   Publication of Ministry of Foreign Affairs (China Division) Brief on CPEC Islamabad, Pakistan. Although no date is given but content shows that it was published sometimes in 2021.

7   India is providing subsidised electricity to its factories whereas Pakistan has been stopped from doing so under IMF conditionalities.

8   Irfan Shahzad Takalvi, '8 years of CPEC: 8 key Outcomes and Beyond' *PIVOT* volume 3, Issue 3, 1 July 2021

9   Mirza Ikhtiar Baig, 'CPEC Herald of Development and Innovation' *PIVOT* vol 3, Issue 3, 1 July 2021

10   'Long-Term Plan of China-Pakistan Economic Corridor', NDRC and CDB December 2015 P.7 to 16

11   Ibid P 14

12   A China state company has expressed concern over the delay in launching the 600 MW solar power project. 300 MW part of 900 MW project has already been completed. Dawn 8th OCT, 2021.

13   http://www.researchgate.net

14   The task was given to Exxon Mobil soon after PTI government came to power. Their earlier assessments were positive on the basis of which PM promised good news for the nation. However, Exxon Mobil did not achieve success. Dawn 18 May, 2021.

15   http//dailytimes.com.pk

16   Chinese engineers were attacked and killed at the site of Dasu Dam early in 2021. An Indian terrorist (serving naval officer working for RAW) was arrested red handed in Pakistan in 2016.

17   Foreign sponsored terrorist were active in Pakistan during US occupation of Afghanistan. TTP became active in Swat and played havoc with the emerald mines. Lacking technology and skills they adopted crude measures like conducting blasts in the emerald mines wasting a lot of this rare stone. The rocks carrying emerald were then smuggled to India. Money earned by terrorists further prolonged the terrorist spell.

18   Dawn, 26 September, 2021.

19   India has been building dams on rivers allocated to Pakistan under the Indus-Basin Agreement. Due to this policy of 'water terrorism' India has already deprived Pakistan of 25% of its share of water.

20   The Seed Bill of 1976 was amended in 2014.

Government and all opposition parties worked together to pass the bill. It paved the way for big international companies in the GM field to takeover agriculture. It is expected that the yield will increase but the country will become dependent on these companies. Implications for human health have not been factored in. Pakistan could also lose its markets in some developed states.

21 One afternoon many years ago I was having lunch at Karachi University Canteen. A young faculty member from BioTechnology Department joined me. Discussion drifted to Biological Warfare. According to her India could launch bio attack against our rural economy. US has already used these tactics against Cuba and North Korea.

22 Bangladesh switched over to underground water soon after 1971 thinking it would be cleaner. This water had high content of Arsenic which had adverse impact on public health. In Pakistan also there are cases of leather tanneries and other industries discharging their waste products in lakes and rivers.

23 NDRC-CDB Report 2015 P20

24 Dawn (Karachi) 15 May, 2017.

25 Dr Xiaoquing Xin director China-Pakistan Economic Corridor Research Centre, threw light on the entire spectrum of cooperation between China and Pakistan under CPEC.

26 Dr Xie mentioned that selected universities from the two countries will collaborate to promote CPEC.

27 Dr Shahida Wizarat, 'Are Resource Abundant Countries Afflicted by the Resource Curse?' *International Journal of Development and Conflict*, 4 (2014) pp 24-39

28 The deal signed with Tethyan Copper Company a joint venture company of Barrick Gold (Canada)

and Antofagasta Minerals (Chile) is a typical example. Baluchistan government was unable to protect its interest due to lack of negotiating skills and corruption of some officials. Situation is not much different in other cases.

29 CPEC Western, Central and Eastern Routes construction status overview, 25 May, 2017, timesofislamabad.com

30 Khurram Shahzad, 'The Eastern, Western and Central Routes of CPEC, batieghar.com (A Weekly of Islamabad) 29 April, 2017.

31 A study of developmental projects in India revealed that the problem is prevalent in India as well.

32 CM of KPK gave statement accusing Federal Government of cheating provinces. Dawn (Karachi) 19 October, 2016.

33 "Mengal likens CPEC to Kalabagh Dam" Dawn (Karachi) 5 September, 2016

34 It was not a CPEC project and negligence on the part of Baluchistan government was responsible for the debacle.

35 Dr Shazia Ghani Director BRI and CPEC, SASSI University (Islamabad) stated this in an interview with the author.

36 Dawn 6 November, 2021

37 Dawn 18 September, 2021

38 US General Votel in a congressional hearing described Russia as a revisionist power accusing it of providing weapons to Afghan Taliban, Dawn (Karachi) 31 March, 2017.

39 After liberation of Afghanistan the Taliban government found documentary evidence of Indian involvement which has been shared with Pakistan according to my information.

40 "Iran keen to join CPEC" Dawn (Karachi) 27 January, 2017.

41 Chahbahar was built by India to trade with Afghanistan and CARs bypassing Pakistan. Now Afghanistan-India trade ties have lost some of their vigor and Iran wants a linkage between Gwadar and Chahbahar.

CHAPTER IV

Karakoram: Highway To Heaven

Karakoram Highway (KKH) also known as 'eighth wonder'[1] of the world is a monument of friendship between China and Pakistan. According to most historical accounts KKH closely follows one of the several tracks of ancient silk route running through the region. It was also a route through which ideas, religions and cultures traveled to impact other societies. Human civilisation evolved as a result of interaction between people of various regions which lay on the silk route.

Karakoram is a Turkic term meaning 'black gravel' the name given to Karakorum pass by Central Asian traders. Other merchants and traders using the route running through mountain ranges called it Muztagh or Ice Mountain. During British occupation of the South Asian subcontinent the region acquired tremendous significance. Around this region three empires seemed to converge.

129

The Chinese empire was the oldest, the Russian empire was in the process of consolidating itself in Central Asia and the British wanted to expand their empire beyond Gilgit as far as possible. The Russian and British empires regarded each other as arch rivals. The 'Great Game' had two objectives i.e to keep the rival powers in check and to exploit every opportunity to expand one's own influence.

After the emergence of Pakistan, freedom movement in Kashmir also gained momentum. Before India could introduce its army to suppress the Kashmiri resistance movement, or take the issue to the Security Council the people of Gilgit-Baltistan and Hunza (together called Northern Areas) defeated the Dogra forces and drove them out. They decided to join Pakistan paving the way for really momentous political developments of the twenty first century. As far back as 1949 the idea of an all-weather road linking Pakistan with its Northern Areas existed, but in 1959 the Government of Pakistan decided to extend Indus Highway, from Hasan Abadal to Islamabad the new capital city.

On 2 March, 1963 after signing of boundary agreement and actual demarcation of boundary in 1964 a new chapter in Pakistan-China relations was opened[2].

The actual task of boundary demarcation was done by a committee composed of Chinese and Pakistani experts. Interesting details of negotiating phase have emerged which show that the diplomatic environment during the negotiations was very congenial. To give an example the grazing ground used by people of a border village for their cattle was somehow shown to be on Chinese side. When the Chinese side were informed of the predicament faced by Pakistani villagers, they readily agreed to alter the map.

After all the pre requisites were provided for, the task of extending the highway from Islamabad to Kashgar began in real earnest. On Pakistan side Pakistan Army played a pivotal role in completing the project. The task of surveying the region and then constructing the road was under the control of Pak army. The federal government entrusted the task to C-in-C Pakistan Army. A new department 'Frontier Works Organization' (FWO) had to be created. It exists even today and is primarily responsible for construction work. During the construction of KKH it worked with Chinese engineers and gained valuable experience. At this stage we also need to recall the contribution made by Pakistan Airforce. They ran sorties day and night carrying personnel and equipment. The work on Chinese side was done by Chinese workers, supervisors and engineers.

Constructing KKH was not an easy venture as the work was being done at an elevation of four thousand seven hundred and fourteen meters, which is equivalent to fifteen thousand four hundred and sixty-six feet. It is the highest paved road in the world and is therefore also known as 'roof of the world[3].'

From Hasan Abdal to Xinjiang in China the total length of KKH was 1300 km. It passes through Gilgit. Now KKH has been connected to the deep sea port of Gwadar in Baluchistan province which has added to its length.

There are two versions regarding the birth of the idea leading to KKH. According to one, General Sher Ali and Pakistan's ambassador General Raza played crucial role in initiating the process. The two of them had a meeting with Chinese Premier Chou Enlai soon after the Pakistan-India war of 1965. When ambassador Raza thanked the Chinese government for their support during the war, he was told that China would have done much more in support of Pakistan had the means been there. Pakistan a longtime ally of US had been facing an arms embargo since the start of 1965 war. At this difficult juncture China offered arms to Pakistan, but the latter was required to make arrangements for transportation. According to the Chinese authorities, it would not be feasible for China to send the consignment through the sea route, due to threat from US navy. Using the air route would have been expensive and till that point, there was no dependable land route between China and Pakistan[4].

A few years prior to this development China had informed Pakistan that it was considering the extension of one of the roads in the Xinjiang region right upto the border with Pakistan. If Pakistan could do the same on its side of the border the two neighbouring countries could have direct land access to each other[5]. Both these ideas suggest that China visualized the significance of a land link between the two countries.

The second version was narrated by Mr Ghulam Farooq an important member of President Ayyub's cabinet. He was also Defense Advisor to the President. According to his account, he suggested the opening of a land route to PM Chou Enlai, in order to promote Chinese trade through Karachi. This would reduce the distance between China and its markets in the Middle East. In my opinion all these versions are based on reality viewed from different angles. These ideas suggest that both sides strongly felt the need for establishment of a land linkage and were rather eager to implement the projects as soon as possible.

In 1967 China worked with Pakistan to develop three roads in the border region. The most important of these was KKH which was inaugurated in 1978. The other two connected Azad Kashmir and the Northern Areas with Xinjiang in China[6]. The Karakoram Range has three passes i.e Mintaka pass, Karakoram pass and Khunjrab pass. It was Pakistan's desire to build KKH through Mintaka pass as it was a comparatively easier option.

This was also part of recommendations made by Major Jafer Ali in his four page report. The report suggested that the road up to Misgar could follow the ancient silk route. There will have to be extensive blasting in the Mintaka pass region which was rather steep. This could pose enormous problems. Another important recommendation was that Batura glacier should be avoided and to achieve this objective two bridges could be made on Hunza river[7]. However, the Chinese authorities wanted to avoid Mintaka pass for strategic reasons.

Ultimately the two sides decided to give due weightage to strategic factors, the KKH as we know passes through Khunjrab pass. The Khunjrab pass due to its difficult terrain, posed a huge challenge particularly for Pakistan side, which had comparatively less experience of building roads in mountainous regions. Keeping the terrain in mind it was decided that the road construction should be undertaken simultaneously at both ends i.e Khunjrab as well as Gilgit[8].

Another issue which required considerable debate and discussion concerned the time factor. Pakistan team members believed that considering all the factors the project would take at least three years to complete. On the other hand the Chinese side was of the view that it should take no more than one year. After much discussion the negotiators found a compromise solution; the project was to be completed in two years. What was not clearly anticipated at the time was financial constrain which forced the Pakistan side to revise the time schedule much against their will. It took five years to complete the project; the delay though regrettable was beyond the control of the government of Pakistan[9].

Projects of this nature are best accomplished in phases. Since both sides were eager to open the linkage at the earliest it was decided to complete a single track first. Traffic from one side had to be stopped in order to let the other side pass. It was obvious that this system would not last for long. The second phase was lunched resulting in further expansion of KKH. During the expansion phase a landslide resulted in halting work. As an after effect of the landslide a lake appeared in the middle of the highway at Atta Abad[10]. This was something quite unanticipated, it led to a number of consequences. All the goods had to be off loaded from trucks and mounted on boats to cross the Atta Abad Lake, off loaded once again to be put on trucks on the other side of the lake in order to continue the journey.

The delay caused due to the lake impeded commercial activities. A solution had to be found which came in the form of a twenty two km long tunnel under the lake. Now commercial activities are gaining momentum as a result of timely solution of the problem. KKH is now a four-lane road, at some points there are six lanes. It is considered to be an all-weather road but there are instances when weather conditions, or landslides lead to temporary closure of the road. KKH enters China a few kilometers north of Gilgit, the Chinese call the section on their side China National Highway 314.

The KKH has been connected to all the provinces of Pakistan. The road networks to serve CPEC run from north to south and east to west. The plan is to create an impressive web of roads, railway lines and oil/gas pipelines running parallel to KKH.

The Western route connecting Pakistan and China is the shortest, it connects Gwadar through KP and Gilgit to Kashgar in Xinjiang. The Eastern route connecting Baluchistan, Sindh and Punjab with KP and Northern Areas is the longest. The central route is comparatively shorter than the eastern one. All routes converge at Gilgit. The Silk Road of ancient times and KKH of today overlap each other at many points. They were created for specific purposes though they often carried unintended consequences. It would not be wrong to say that routes are intricately connected to history. They move history forward but under certain circumstances they also seem to hold it hostage. Routes may occur naturally or they may be created as a result of human endeavor. In the past rivalries led to efforts to control trade routes thereby causing conflicts as they do even now. In this sense political interactions and the processes influencing them have not changed much.

Working together to open a modern route in the form of KKH brought China and Pakistan even closer. Carving out roads in mountains at such a high altitude is a great feat of engineering highly regarded by professionals. About 887 km of the road is on Pakistani side of the border and around 413 km on the Chinese side. Hundreds of workers on both sides of the border sacrificed their lives to turn this dream into reality. Pakistanis learnt a lot from rich Chinese experience in carving out roads in mountain regions. Chinese also provided construction equipment which was different from what Pakistanis had used in the past, but that did not pose too much of a problem. The sweat and blood of Chinese and Pakistani workers created 'a wonder of the world' in the form of KKH.[11]

There is an interesting story narrated in 'History of Karakoram Highway' regarding how KKH got its name. Major General Jamil ud Din Faruqi was busy working on the project surrounded by maps when one of the staff officers asked him about the name of the road. 'Karakoram Highway, yes that is the name'[12] Chinese foreign minister Marshal Chen Yi gave it an even more interesting name. At a dinner party when he rose to speak he said, "It is a Friendship Highway you are going to build it with your troops and labourers. Least we can do is to provide you the equipment."[13]

Socio-Economic Impact of KKH

The construction of KKH has made a lot of difference in the lives of common people living in the Northern Areas of Pakistan. Those who visited Gilgit-Baltistan (GB) and Hunza before KKH was constructed and have had the chance to visit the areas now see a world of difference. There were a number of features which had to be taken into account while formulating social development policy for the region. The terrain is extremely difficult and due to negligence of the British rulers there was no public transport system available, mobility was a big issue. Another hurdle retarding development was demography of the region. The villages were small and scattered due to which providing educational and other facilities in every village was not easy. Job opportunities were nonexistent and agricultural land available to families was too small and fragmented. The weather conditions were harsh and food security a distant dream.

The administration was in the hands of the British Political Agent, whose main worry was to consolidate British control over the region. The British were least concerned about the welfare of the local people. After independence the government of Pakistan created blue print for constructing an all-weather road, but it took more than ten years to implement the project. The biggest challenge facing the government was to improve the facilities available to people of this strategic region. A number of people I interviewed were of the view that a peaceful and silent revolution has taken over the region since the construction of KKH.

When the army was constructing KKH they started offering medical and educational facilities to people living around the route of KKH. This was not a permanent arrangement, the idea being that while the army was deployed in the region, people should get as much benefit as possible. Situation started improving after KKH was built and a network of link roads was provided.

The Government of Pakistan has exempted the people of Northern Areas from direct taxes, basic food items like wheat flour, powdered milk, sugar and kerosene are subsidised by the government. Transportation cost is also covered by the government[14]. According to Kreutzmann 'Northern Areas Transport Corporation' was founded in 1974. It provided much needed connectivity to people besides creating jobs. A linkage between KKH and the Grand Trunk Road opened up many options for the people of Northern Areas.

Promotion of educational facilities became possible only after KKH and connecting road networks opened up the region. There is substantial evidence to suggest that economic and social developments follow promotion of education. Only after literacy rate achieves a certain level can the society hope for economic and social change.

In 1976-78 Directorate of Education was established. In 1979 Ministry of Kashmir Affairs was given control of the educational system. The Government of Pakistan's interest in promoting education in

Norther Areas could be gauged from the fact that a large number of institutions were established during 1970s and 1980s. 'Agha Khan Educational Services Pakistan, has always played a laudable role in promoting education particularly in the Northern Areas. National Educational Foundation and the private sector have also played their part in promoting education.

In 1981 the literacy rate was 14% which increased to 52% by 2005, five fold increase in twenty four years. Another encouraging factor is increase in enrollment in schools and colleges. Female literacy is also on the rise which has been a source of encouragement for all.

In 2002 Karakoram International University was established.[15] It has impressive infrastructure and efforts are under way to attract highly qualified faculty. There is scope for expansion in future, in terms of new fields of study to be introduced, expansion of infrastructure for research and faculty development. The idea is to provide world class educational facilities and to share them with local and foreign students particularly from the region.

Where local expertise is available, institutions will draw human resource from the local talent pool. However, it will take time for local talent pool to grow, during this phase talent from the rest of the country can be utilized. Initially when school system was in the process of expansion, school teachers from all parts of the country were selected on merit and their efforts won acclaim. Young people from Northern Areas have opportunities waiting for them in big cities of Pakistan and it seems that they are keen to utilize them.

The population of Northern Areas has shown steady increase. There is pressure on existing facilities. The local and federal governments are trying to promote health facilities. In this field too Aga khan Foundation is playing a prominent role. Clinics and hospitals have been established in the last few decades but when seriously ill patients have to be shifted to bigger hospitals, which are a few miles away and time is of essence, it still poses a challenge for the family and hospital staff.

Another serious problem is shortage of doctors because even local doctors prefer to work in hospitals in big cities as there are more learning opportunities there. Sometimes Lady Health Visitors and Lady Health Workers try to bridge the gap, but they are trained for a specific purpose which does not include treatment of ailing people[16]. Attempts are underway to reduce child and mother mortality rates. Family Planning is another area of growing interest at government and private levels.

Out migration of young males in particular is becoming a permanent feature of life in Northern Areas. With ease of travel many young people leave their homes for higher education or better job opportunities. It has opened new avenues of progress for local people and, due to remittances the families are also financially better off.

As far as agriculture and resource development are concerned people of Northern Areas are no longer dependent on locally produced items. They get regular supply of subsidized wheat, rice, milk and vegetables from other provinces of Pakistan. Eating habits have changed, food items which people would not have eaten in the past are becoming part of diet, with passage of time they are gaining popularity. Interviews with local people suggest that even status symbols have changed; in the past material possessions and financial assets determined social standing of a person. This may still be true in some cases but in most cases especially among younger population level of education, name of university and academic achievements have acquired greater importance.

As a result of construction of KKH and link roads local people have many new avenues. Land trade between China and Pakistan has been increasing steadily, although it is much less than the potential which exists. With research and proper planning, it can grow in future. Northern Areas Trading Corporation (NATC) came into being in 1968. Gilgit is the centre of activity of NATC. Under this arrangement local shareholders have a platform to work together.

Entrepreneurs from Northern Areas are striving hard to benefit from opportunities which exist now. Pakistan's various provinces offer leather and leather goods, cotton, medicines, tobacco and other items. The Northern Areas can carve out a niche for themselves as there is market for goods like woolen cloth, dried apricots, almonds, walnuts and other dry fruits which are locally produced. The Hunzukuts have friends and family on the Chinese side of the border, these ties have now been revived as travel has become easier[17].

The region has mineral wealth which if properly organized can add to public welfare. Ruby mines need to be developed. People should be trained to properly extract the precious stone, refine and polish it. Jewelry industry can be promoted creating a lot of job opportunities. Resources like China clay and marble can play a role in promoting development, but due to non-availability of cheap electricity progress has been slow.

Smuggling of timber and firewood should be controlled in order to curtail adverse impact on the environment[18]. Travel between Northern Areas and other parts of Pakistan has become much cheaper and easier. As already mentioned, young people travel to various parts of Pakistan in order to study or gain employment. This is not a one-way traffic as many Pakistani and foreign tourists head to Northern Areas during summer months.

Many local people are making their livelihood from tourism. It would not be an exaggeration to say that the prospects for promoting prosperity, have increased. The economic condition of local population has improved tremendously. A new class of professionals and entrepreneurs has emerged, more people have been pulled out of poverty compared to the past. Inter marriages have started taking place which was unheard of in yester years[19].

Geo-economic and Strategic Dimension of KKH

The construction of an all-weather road in the Karakoram region has enabled China and Pakistan to further strengthen their relationship. Centuries old trade relations and Silk Route cooperation has been revived under twenty first century framework. Under the new conditions both countries suffer from certain vulnerabilities. It is in the interest of both neighboring states to give practical shape to their relationship in order to enhance their mutual security.

China felt threatened after the emergence of Sino-Soviet rivalry. It was not just an ideological challenge emanating from Soviet Union, there was an obvious geo-strategic threat which could not be over-looked by China. The China-Soviet border was 7,524 kilometer long. There was threat posed by Soviet fleet present in Vladivostok. In case of a blockade launched by Soviet Navy, China could face a serious situation[20]. The Indians were keen to take advantage of this situation. They had un-demarcated border with China; India launched hostilities against Chinese forces in the border area in 1962. According to British journalist Neville Maxwell, Indians provoked China to launch a war in 1962. For this he has blamed Nehru's Forward Policy.[21] They hoped to achieve US military support as a result of this policy. As a matter of fact India succeeded in achieving Western support along with Soviet support. Vietnam an ally also turned against China. China felt encircled and vulnerable; it was important to break this feeling of encirclement as soon as possible[22].

After the construction of KKH the encirclement was broken, China got access to a new route. The existence of this new route further strengthened friendly ties between the two countries.

Pakistan also found itself in a precarious situation. India was the biggest threat to Pakistan's security. India tried to take over princely states by force since many of them were reluctant to join India. This policy applied to Kashmir as well and, in spite of Security Council resolutions in favour of holding plebiscite, India sent its forces in and was able to take over two thirds of Kashmir. India was four times bigger than Pakistan at that time, but after India took control of East Pakistan and created Bangladesh that gap has become even bigger.

India has so far fought three wars against Pakistan. Pakistan joined US sponsored military alliances hoping to ward off Indian military pressure. It had no idea that US would ditch it soon. In 1962 US gave India military equipment and support despite Pakistan's opposition. In 1965 war against India, Pakistan would have faced dire consequence had China not supported it. The US placed an arms embargo against both countries, but Pakistan suffered more as it was more dependent on US weapons.

Soviet Union was antagonized when Pakistan joined CENTO and SEATO, therefore, it too supported India in both the wars. Relations with Afghanistan were far from friendly as it laid claim to Pakistani territory refusing to accept the Durand Line. In collusion with India and Soviet Union it launched the Pakhunistan stunt. These were serious threats for the security of Pakistan, the country needed a dependable ally in the region, who would stand by it in times of need. This became possible practically after KKH was constructed.

It was due to this background that President Ayyub remarked 'that in order of priority the first urgency of the highway was strategic and one of immediate significance'. The second objective was economic and commercial importance of the highway i.e the opening up of an inaccessible region and the establishment of a land route to the adjoining country.[23] It was due to strategic factors that the project was given priority and great urgency was attached to it at every stage. This is one aspect which has been criticized by Brigadier (retired) Muhammad Mumtaz Khalid the author of History of

Karakoram Highway[24]. Using these arguments as a base some other scholars have also been critical of the haste which marked official approach to KKH[25].

In 1965 war China provided valuable support to Pakistan, but Chinese authorities maintained that they could have done much more had the land link been there. Some experts of China-Pakistan relations express surprise that China did not effectively use KKH to support Pakistan in 1971 War against India. There are three factors which should be kept in mind while analyzing China's approach, i) The road was not fully operational, some portions of the road were still under construction. It was not possible to use them for heavy traffic, ii) although KKH is an all-weather road but while it was under construction it was probably not an easy task to ply heavy vehicles in winter months, iii) Soviet Union signed a Treaty of Security and Cooperation with India as it was fearful of the rising power of China. It wanted a pretext to attack China and prevent or at least delay the emergence of China as a major power.

The fifty-year period since then has added to China's power, enhanced its confidence in the last couple of decades and, truly placed it in the category of a major world power. As CPEC and other tracks of BRI gain momentum China's economy will become even stronger. China has simultaneously launched military modernization programme which is progressing well.

Another strategic benefit of KKH for Pakistan also needs to be taken into account. Northern Areas and Azad Kashmir are more closely integrated into Pakistan now. This will prove to be a great asset in future. The people of these two areas are benefitting directly from the availability of this trade route. It has promoted a silent revolution in these regions and, the people enjoy a much higher level of prosperity, than they ever did in the past. In case of a threat from an adversary China and Pakistan will be in a much better position to respond to the challenge.

KKH's strategic and geo-economic value has been further enhanced due to the establishment of deep-sea port at Gwadar. Some US and Indian strategists are of the view that China will use Gwadar as a naval base. There is very little substance in this assertion, as China has not shown much interest in establishing military bases in foreign countries. In this sense Chinese policy is very different compared to US. The Chinese emphasis is on promoting commercial and economic activity. Secondly, the agreement between Pakistan and China regarding Gwadar does not carry a military clause. However, if China and Pakistan perceive that a military threat is emerging, which could jeopardize their security and economic wellbeing, then the idea of cooperating to establish a naval base might acquire credence.

The success of Chinese policy of developing Xinjiang and other adjoining areas depends largely on this route. KKH and Gwadar connect Western China with its trading partners in Middle East and Africa. Goods manufactured in Western China will have markets in Middle East and Africa. Energy and raw materials for factories in the region will follow the same route. This is the shortest possible trade route for China and many of its trading partners.

Pakistan too has adopted the policy of developing its least developed areas, in order to bring them at par with comparatively more developed regions. The CPEC can facilitate this objective and promote better integration of various provinces of Pakistan. The Indian sponsored terrorist movement in Baluchistan and other provinces of Pakistan will be easier to control.[26] Similarly the US supported separatist movement against China could also be defeated[27].

CPEC is known as a game changer in Pakistan apart from providing a trade route to China. The KKH and Gwadar route can also facilitate Central Asian states and Afghanistan. The entire corridor can serve as the back bone of Pakistan's economy. All along the CPEC route industrial units are being developed along with Special Economic Zones (SEZs). Another important dimension of CPEC is promotion of agriculture. It is planned that along the highway's agricultural farms and agricultural research units will be established. Near Gwadar some oil refineries and at least one SEZ will also be established. Oil pipelines running from Gwadar to

Western China (particularly Xinjiang) are integral part of CPEC. Russia has experience of laying oil and gas pipelines; it has already expressed interest in participating in these ventures.

It was expected that as time passed KKH which was seen as an asset of strategic nature, would show it's commercial and economic dimensions. This expectation turned out to be true, Pakistan has decided to use its geo-strategic location to promote economic development. In the past during the Cold War US benefitted from Pakistan's location for military purposes. China's orientation is different, its main focus is on promoting commercial and economic activities for mutual benefit. This provides Pakistan with an opportunity for long term economic development and poverty alleviation. If CPEC develops according to the plan and opposition can be neutralized, Pakistan could emerge as a hub of regional trade. Its economy would be stabilized and this would have positive impact on its domestic politics and foreign policy.

Threats to Karakoram Highway: Way Forward

KKH is a symbol of China-Pakistan friendship, probably for this reason states wanting to curtail China's growing influence, and those wanting to restrict Pakistan's prospects of economic development, have been hostile to this trade route[28]. According to one account at the time of inauguration of KKH, Chinese Vice-Premier Geng

Biao remarked, that now China would be in a better position to supply heavy military equipment to Pakistan in times of need[29].

KKH is mostly viewed in the strategic context by many states particularly the US, European states and India; this too gives rise to apprehensions regarding KKH. It has set into motion a strong propaganda machinery which knows no limits. According to Ziad Haider[30] KKH is instrumental in promoting everything from political Islam, drugs and HIV/AIDs. Another author Hasnain Kazim has made claims which suggest that KKH is perhaps the most dangerous road to travel on.[31] It is true that mountain roads do carry some element of risk but KKH is no more dangerous than any other mountain highway. It had to be closed down on certain occasions due to a landslide or heavy rains. However, I doubt there is any mountain road which has been free of these problems.

Basically two types of problems afflict the KKH; there are issues which are indigenous in nature. The environmentalists are gaining strength in Pakistan due to freedom enjoyed by the media. They are concerned about environmental consequences of KKH which are always assumed to be negative. It is true that in the beginning when work was initiated a lot of blasting had to be done, which carried many unintended consequences like cracks which appeared in the mountains. At times it caused accidents which received media attention. Besides, trees had to be cut during construction and expansion of the highway.

The environmentalists did not raise any objections then but now they are gaining strength. Another apprehension which they have is that, gradually when trade picks up and there are hundreds of trucks and other vehicles, plying on this highway pollution will increase many fold. Since there will be oil/gas pipelines running along the highway in case of an accident there will be a much bigger disaster than anyone can foresee today.

Although environmentalists have a point and some government officials I talked to, tried to convince me that now all the departments concerned, follow very stringent code for protection of environment. NOC from relevant departments is an essential requirement without which nothing can be done. It was also claimed by them that government on regular basis seeks advice from experts and NGOs. However, there has to be a balance between developmental needs and prevention of pollution. No government in the world can afford to adopt simplistic approach, opting for environment at the expense of development or vice versa. A healthy balance has to be maintained, because public health is a top priority at all times, but creating economic opportunities is also an important consideration.

Some NGOs in the name of creating awareness have often tried to use people, against provincial and federal government schemes/plans to promote development. This would not seem too objectionable had the NGOs been funded by sources from within the country. However, most of the NOGs draw their funds from the same countries that have been opposing KKH, BRI and CPEC. This is a concern which has been expressed also by people belonging to civil society.

Another serious issue is the tendency shown by some groups to block KKH under slightest pretext. In this case past governments and the current one should also share responsibility. I met people long time back who claimed, they had not been paid compensation for the loss of homes, which they suffered when KKH was constructed and later when it was expanded. One such group blocked the highway for quite a long time and left only after government agreed to look into their grievances. In 2014 once again a group of people blocked KKH as they did not like federal government's policy of withdrawing subsidy on wheat. They vacated their positions only when a committee was formed to resolve Gilgit wheat subsidy issue[32]. More recently the people once again blocked KKH for hours claiming that the wheat supplied to Gilgit was of low quality[33].

It makes one wonder whether these actions are spontaneous or pre planned in which case who is planning it and for what purpose? It has been happening too often and sometimes on flimsy grounds. Some officials believe that people know the importance of KKH and they are in a position to exploit it in order to push their agenda. Others are of the view that adversaries of the country could be working behind the scene. It is not difficult for well-trained foreign intelligence agencies to orchestrate local elements in a subtle manner. In any case this sort of situation sends a wrong signal to friends and foes alike; the government needs to take local leadership into confidence. The battle for hearts and minds of people is on, whoever wins this battle will be in a position to call the shots.

As already pointed out US and India along with some other states have adopted a rather hostile posture against KKH, BRI and CPEC (which is regarded as an important component of BRI). US discomfort derives from growing Chinese influence. In 2021 according to one account China achieved the status of being largest economy in some economic indicators at global level having left US behind in some areas[34]. China's economic power is expected to grow even more after BRI becomes fully operational. US wants to prevent or delay that from happening.

India is even more afraid of China's growing economic and military might. It is believed that when India launched its road construction project in Galwan river valley in Ladakh in 2020, China read Indian intentions. Indian plans were to build infrastructure right upto the point where it could cut off KKH. China could not allow that to happen. On 15th and 16th June in 2020 the short military engagement between China and India resulted in the latter's defeat.

The questions now confronting Pakistani strategists are simple but unfortunately there are no easy answers. Will the adversaries opt for a full-fledged military conflict? If they do so what are the chances of it leading to a nuclear show down. If we look towards history for guidance, it will suggest that normally states follow pragmatism. States often resort to brinkmanship but they also know, that if they allow things to go beyond a certain level, the situation might spiral out of their hands. Even if adversaries desist from pursuing outright conventional military conflict it does not mean that hostilities will not be initiated.

Limited use of military force in combination with other methods, has been relied upon by many states in the past and with good results. During world war II, Britain used it extensively in Europe and Asia against its adversaries. US tried this method against Cuba, when CIA trained Cuban immigrants were infiltrated into Cuba. This was done in early 1960s to foment trouble against the Socialist government. US failed in its efforts against Cuba but CIA successfully used these methods against several Latin American states. During Kissinger years 'Death Squads' were used by CIA to kill young people suspected of being Communist.

India also extensively used terrorism to break up Pakistan in 1971. In more recent times India tried to use the same method against Pakistan but this time Baluchistan, parts of Sindh and KPK were their main targets. They used US occupied Afghanistan and Iranian territory (Chahbahar) for this purpose. Apart from Kulbhushan Jadhav other Indians have also been arrested. From the revelations made by Kulbhushan it is obvious that he was not just a spy he was promoting acts of terrorism. It is clear that India was targeting the entire route of CPEC. Had KKH been paralyzed it would have frozen CPEC.

On 23rd June 2013 terrorists attacked foreign tourists in Nanga Parbat area killing ten tourists and their guide[35]. It was for the first time that terrorists struck there. A few aspects of this act of terrorism are noteworthy, firstly the terrorists were operating from US occupied Afghanistan where CIA and RAW were given a free hand. Secondly, the attack took place in close proximity to KKH which suggests that perhaps both KKH and CPEC were targets of the attackers.

This was part of psychological warfare, as people's confidence in Security arrangements in the region, was undermined for quite some time. Media all over the world splashed the news which highlighted the security problem depicting Pakistan as an insecure state. Pakistan's economy was another casualty of this act of terrorism, as after this mountaineering expeditions remained suspended for quite some time. Before this attack Pakistan was the most popular destination for mountaineering expeditions. Tourism was badly hit and the country continued to suffer for a long time. Image counts a lot in the age of media, it seemed like all the anti-CPEC (and anti-KKH) forces turned their attention on tarnishing Pakistan's image. If a country's image is ruined the economy automatically collapses.

The ethnic and sectarian composition of the region has been diverse. People of all ethnicities and sectarian identities have been living peacefully for centuries without any problem. Even Hindu traders were not discriminated against by local people. Pakistani Shias were in the forefront of struggle for independence they actively participate in all walks of national life. The vast majority are peace loving people but attempts were made by RAW and other hostile intelligence agencies, to ignite sectarian and ethnic conflict in the Northern Areas in particular. Hodge attributes this to the Islamic Revolution in Iran in 1979.

There is an assumption that the revolution by itself heightened sectarian tension. However, there is no evidence presented by him in this regard. On the other hand ethnic and sectarian organizations operating in Pakistan were being funded by RAW operating from US occupied Afghanistan. After US withdrawal a lot of documents which fell in the hands of Afghan Taliban established this point. The documents discovered by new Government of Afghanistan in border areas have probably been shared with Pakistan. MQM (London), Baluch Liberation army and other Baluch terrorist groups, Pakistani Taliban and some sectarian groups were drawing funds from Indian agencies operating from occupied Afghanistan's border areas with Pakistan[36].

Now India (like the US) has been forced out of Afghanistan and the network created by them has almost collapsed. Iran too was approached by China to adopt a more positive approach towards CPEC. Iran found India's efforts to build road network connecting Chahbahar with Northern border of Iran too slow. Now the project has been taken away from India. Chahbahar which was being used by India, as a spy and terror sponsoring centre against Pakistan, will probably refrain from playing this role.

It will not be easy for India to launch terrorist operations against Pakistan, from Afghanistan or Iran now. However, the long Pakistan-India border is still available to them. Moreover, they still have their 'Sleeper Cells' in Pakistan, which is why traces of terrorism continued in one form or another, even after Indian and US withdrawal from Afghanistan. This challenge will subside only when the Sleeper Cells are neutralized and infiltration is stopped.

Adversaries want to impede the progress of CPEC at any cost short of an all-out war. Their primary focus will be on fifth generation warfare, included within the frame-work are a number of possibilities. Psychological warfare carried out through the media can be an effective tool against the adversary. Undermining the economy of the target state is also a major dimension of fifth generation warfare. Imposing sanctions of all kinds, restrictions under FATF and other similar methods have been used in the past.

According to Andrew Small, 'KKH has altered the balance of geography and politics on the subcontinent'. Due to this reason opposition to the strategic highway will continue to grow in future.[37] China and Pakistan need to further enhance their cooperation in technological and intelligence gathering sectors. The intelligence agencies should be strengthened, the government should be able to anticipate if trouble is brewing in the region. The objective should be to redress problems before adversaries use them to their advantage. Effort should be made to win over the people, their grievances should be removed through good governance. The people should be made to realize that blockading KKH for any reason will be detrimental to their own interest.

Chapter IV

1   Brigadier (Retd) Muhammad Mumtaz Khalid, History of Karakoram Highway vol II, (Hamza Pervez Printers, Rawalpindi 2009). p 21 Mention has been made of Lt. Col Mujtaba Zahir Kidwai's Memoirs of KKH

2   Ibid P.7

3   Andrea Thompson, The Real Story Behind the 'Roof of the World' https://www.livescience.com Also see Journey to the roof of the world, The Nation 7 September, 2014, https://nation.com.pk

4   *Karakoram Highway*, Opcit P2.

5   Ibid P.1

6   Ghulam Ali, *China-Pakistan Relations a Historical Analysis*, (Oxford University Press Karachi 2017) pp 68-69

7   *History of Karakoram Highway*, opcit pp12-14.

8   Ibid p.16

9   Ibid p23

10 It has now become a picnic spot. The lake area is scenic and peaceful.

11 On Pakistani side civilian workers also participated in the project as it was more economical to employ them.

12 *History of Karakoram Highway* p17

13 Ibid

14 Hermann Kreutzmann, 'The Karakoram Highway: The Impact of Road Construction on Mountain Societies', (Modern Asian studies October 1991). p724

15 In my interviews with people who go regularly to KIU to attend seminars it emerged that the university is coming up as a great regional centre of academic excellence. It enjoyes all the modern facilities.

16 Aga Khan Foundation is doing good work in education and health sectors particularly in Northern Areas. Filling the gaps is a challenge but efforts are on to bring about improvement.

17 Kreutzmann, opcit p725

18 Ibid p733

19 Some of my colleagues who regularly visit the region say that the pace of these changes has been fast. The last twenty or twenty five years have been important in this sense.

20 *History of KKH*, opcit p8

21 Neville Maxwell, *India's China War*, Amazon.com 2015

22 Opcit

23 *History of Karakoram Highway* p22

24 Ibid Ppp 27-56

25 Andrew Small, *The China-Pakistan Axis Asias New Geopoitics,* (Hurst and Company London, 2015). p.105

26 Kulbhushan admitted to creating and supporting secessionist forces in Baluchistan and elsewhere in Pakistan.

27 Some Cubans moved to US after the Socialist revolution in Cuba. The CIA trained them and infiltrated them into Cuba on at least two occasions in 1960s. Some Chinese Scholars I interviewed thought US might be using Chinese who went to US in 1950s. It would be better to use tact rather than force to settle this problem.

28 Anthony E. Hillman, *The Emperors New Road China and the project of the Century* (Yale University Press New Haven 2020). p 134

29 Mehnaz Z. Ispahani, *Roads and Rivals the Politics of Access in the Borderlands of Asia*, (I.B Tauris London 1989). p 200

30 Zaid Hyder, 'Sino-Pakistan Relations and Xinjiang's

Uyghurs. Trade and Islam along the Karakoram Highway', *Asian Survey* vol, 45, No. 4 July/August 2005 p. 529.

31 Hasnain Kazim, The Karakorum Highway: China's Asphalt Power play in Pakistan http://www.spicgel.de/international/world/china-expands-karakoram-highway-to-pakistan-a-844282.html

32 Dawn.com 23 April, 2014.

33 https://www.aninews.in>world>asia 10 December, 2021.

34 http://www.everycrsreport.com

35 Adam Hodge, Karakoram Highway: China's Treacherous Pakistan Corridor.
https://thediplomat.com/2013/07/karakoram-highway-chinas-treacherous-pakistani-corridor/3/

36 In December 2004 Dawn published a report on the front page. It was a report released by Rand Corporation which advised US Government to exploit ethnic and sectarian fault lines in the Muslim world. It further suggested that where these do not exist they can be created. The policy was implemented for the first time in US occupied Iraq.

37 Andrew Small, Opcit p. 106.

CHAPTER V

Special Economic Zones Under Cpec Challenges And Opportunities

Special Economic Zones (SEZs) have become popular in the last three decades. According to ILO in 1986 there were 176 SEZs in 47 countries. The number rose to 3500 in 130 countries within two decades. According to World Investment Report of 2019 the number of SEZs has risen to 5400 which are spread over 147 countries. Millions of people have found employment in these ventures all over the world. [1]

The roots of the system can be traced back to 'agglomeration of industries' which removed the concept of 'space economy' thus transforming the industrial process. Agglomerations were first created in Gibraltar (1704) and Singapore (1819). In 1959 a zone was created in Ireland which is acknowledged as the first "modern zone". A number of new zones have emerged under different names but they are mostly subsumed under the title of Special Economic Zones.[2]

The reason behind the immense popularity of the concept can be traced back to success of several of these ventures particularly in the case of China. The success stories stand out and dominate the narrative thereby overshadowing cases of failure. Since the process started, there have been some cases where challenges proved to be too daunting.[3]

Case studies need to be undertaken in order to explore the factors behind successful ventures and to get a better understanding of challenges which can retard progress. Attempt should also be made to understand the similarities and distinctions under laying various ventures.

SEZs are selected and well demarcated areas of a country where special rules and regulations are implemented in order to attract FDI, create jobs and promote development. The financial and non-financial incentives given in this geographical zone are different from regulations applied in rest of the country. The country retains sovereignty over the territory but often major concessions are given to foreign firms (both public and privately owned).[4] Free Trade Zones (FTZ) are duty free areas also known as commercial free zones. They are fenced off, providing storage and warehousing facilities. Trans-shipment and re-export operations are also facilitated.

Free Ports (FP) are spread over much larger areas. They are designed to facilitate a variety of commercial activities including retail sales, on-site residences are also permitted. Tourism and other activities providing commercial incentives and benefits are provided. The entire port city is within field of operation. Good law and order and infrastructure are a must.

Export Processing Zones (EPZ) are industrial estates producing manufactured goods primarily for export. Since the products are for foreign markets it would help if the taste and culture of the foreign consumers is taken into account[5]. Another important consideration would be the nature of demand and of course availability of suitable infrastructure.

Hybrid EPZs are a more complex group. They have two sub-categories a general zone which is open to all industries. However separate zones may be created to produce specific exportable items. There is some debate within World Bank regarding the role and future of this category of SEZ.

Enterprise Zones (EZs) are normally located in distressed urban or rural areas in order to develop these areas, create jobs and reduce poverty. Special features like tax incentives and other financial inducements are necessary to achieve the stated goal and objectives.

Single Factory EPZs are fairly common. Under this system incentives are provided to individual enterprises and other small business groups to establish factories irrespective of location. There is no specific or fenced off region and the investor has the freedom of choice. Normally small investors benefit more from the scheme. Specialized Zones (SZ) constitute an important category of SEZs. "Science parks" and "technology parks" can be created in order to develop technology and upgrade local skills.

This can also serve as a mechanism for technology transfer to the host country. Petrochemical enterprises, logistic parks and other similar activities can be undertaken.[6] Banking, training, communication networks and transportation services are a vital part of all the zones. They determine the level of success of various zones and one must realise, that success of all these ventures is vitally linked, to the availability of above-mentioned contributing factors. Business parks adjacent to cities also include services like banking, insurance, transportation etc apart from training and communication facilities. Another important feature distinguishing various ventures is mode of ownership. Public sector ownership of infrastructure and services as an incentive to the private sector has been tried with good results.

The public sector by pursuing conducive land policies has often contributed to the process of promoting economic activity. The investors prefer either ownership of land in their use or long-term lease with possibility of renewal. At times renting land on suitable terms is also viewed as a good possibility as it helps reduce initial expenses.

Build-operate-transfer (BOT) and build-own-operate approaches to on-site and off-site zones with government guarantees and or financial support is another approach often followed.

Public sector companies sometimes contract agreements with private sector management firms to fill the management gap. There is an equity-shifting arrangement whereby a private firm can exercise the option of buying a public sector firm on the basis of pre-determined performance criteria.

The above data shows that at least in the case of OIC countries there is a wide variety of options to choose from where mode of ownership is concerned. Other regional states have developed mechanisms best suited to their cases.

Special Economic Zones in China

China started with four zones to gain understanding of market oriented economic reforms.[7] The experimentation with new laws was a complicated process. Taxation system, laws governing market, land, labour, customers, immigration and finance had to be redesigned in order to meet new goals and objectives.

The experience gained from the four zones was valuable, Chinese experience with SEZs, is among the most successful in the world. In the light of lessons learnt China expanded and diversified the whole process and many more SEZs were established all over the country. Gradually the agenda became more sophisticated, whereas initially the main focus was on gaining FDI and creation of employment opportunities. It culminated in desire to establish high technology ventures like science and technology parks. As a result of this exercise there was up-gradation of technical skills leading to increase in GDP and exports. It also contributed to diversification of exports. Industrial parks and technological innovation parks draw their popularity from the fact that they contributed to China's immense progress. According to Zeng these SEZs accounted for 46% exports, 22% of GDP besides generating more than 30 million jobs.

The level of success achieved by China appears to be impressive particularly if it is kept in mind that Chinese system revolved around the concept of centrally planned economy. Adoption of economic reforms in 1978 resulted in Open Door Policy. Proper implementation of reforms ensured success which has been a source of encouragement to other developing states. Patience has been the hallmark of Chinese approach; initially only four

SEZs were created, after gaining experience and acquiring management skills the number of SEZs was increased. They gradually spread to various parts of the country. Choice of location of SEZs is an important consideration, and SEZs now belong to a variety of categories. The SEZs promoting technological innovation are highly encouraged.

The factors leading to success of China in the SEZ sector are several but only a few will be highlighted here. These factors can be divided into four categories i.e Psychological, geographical, economic and political. The mindset is the most important factor, Chinese have a lot of patience, high degree of motivation, flexibility to learn from experience and grip over the other three categories. Meritocracy is encouraged by the Chinese system.

The availability of good quality infrastructure is also of essence. Choice of the location of industry and services determines the level of success. If items produced are for export then proximity to sea ports and airports is required. However, if markets are accessible through land then railway networks and trucking services will be in demand. A combination of land and sea routes is essential to promote trade. Air route is the most expensive but it cannot be entirely ruled out. In the realm of economics, the Chinese planners were ready to think out of box solutions. The innovative economic ideas appeared to be risky in the eyes of some. But as time passed and experience became a dependable guide confidence increased. Open Door policy resulted in impressive flow of FDI. Foreign funding sources developed trust and inhibition gave way to integration.

China's experience with SEZs of all categories has been successful, it would not be wrong to say that it is treated more or less as a role model in this particular area. Other nations wanting to benefit from SEZs have tried to apply lessons learnt from Chinese experience.

Special Economy Zones in Other Regions

Middle Eastern states have generally been successful in creating SEZs. The UAE stands out in this regard. Morocco has gathered good experience over the years and its ability to apply corrective measures, where necessary, has been an asset.

Central Asian states like Kazakhstan started these ventures in 1990s. Higher literacy rate and proximity to China can be counted as plus points but lack of experience in running public-private partnerships was a drawback. Another complicating factor is land locked position which poses formidable challenges, however, BRI has helped these states in a number of ways[8]. With the opening of old trade routes under a new frame-work handicaps like being landlocked will be redressed in future.

South Asian states including Pakistan, India, Bangladesh and Sri Lanka have not only established SEZs they hope to expand them in future. New SEZs are also being planned. SEZs in Sri Lanka, Bangladesh and Maldives are generally successful. In India the SEZs established in Mumbai region have shown better performance compared to Kandla. [9]

East Asian states i.e Philippines, Thailand, Malaysia and Indonesia have shown promise to achieve higher levels of success where SEZs are concerned. A few factors stand out; the state of infrastructure in East Asia is much better compared to most other regions. Another asset is higher literacy rate and work ethics prevalent in the region. Most states in the region as members of ASEAN (which is a very successful regional organization) have learned skills which are conducive to promoting cooperation. The mind-set which has evolved over the years is definitely an asset.

African states on the other hand have been less successful when compared to other regions in terms of performance of SEZs. This trend can be partially attributed to political environment in the region. Civil wars in some states, fear of interstate conflict and the fact that infrastructure is relatively in poor condition have all added up to make the situation complex. The negative role of some Western MNC's has added to confusion. Also the legacy left by colonial powers has not been helpful. Resource curse, exploitative policies of ex-colonial powers, along with other disruptive trends have increased poverty. [10]

To put it in a nutshell the political and economic environments were not conducive for foreign investment. However, more recently a new political phenomenon has emerged. China since the launching of Belt and Road Initiative has become more cognizant of the importance of Africa. Many infrastructure projects have been launched which will play a crucial role in promoting trade and commerce. The combination of African resources and Chinese technology can reverse the negative trends but for this to materialise African states will have to show greater resolve. Africa has much to gain from the process of integration being promoted by China under its Belt and Road Initiative.

Special Economic Zones in Pakistan

Pakistan had Export Processing Zone in Landhi (Karachi) even before CPEC was launched. With a growing population and one of the largest pools of young people under the age of 30, government's desire to create jobs and open new avenues of prosperity is understandable. SEZs of various types have been created. [11]

As in the case of other developing states Pakistan's main objectives in creating various types of SEZs are to attract FDI, promote industrialization, create jobs and create markets abroad for Pakistani manufactured goods. This strategy was successful in diversifying Pakistani exports while increasing the share of manufactured goods in the export matrix[12]. It was also expected to promote prosperity in the state. Industrial Estates (IEs), Export Processing Zones (EPZs), Free Trade Zones (FTZs) and a variety of ventures were launched during 1960s. Statutory Trading Estate was established in 1963. The first EPZ was established in 1989. In 1970s PPP government's focus on nationalization reduced private sectors confidence in Pakistan. Though Zia's government and subsequent political governments came up with privatization policy

S. No	PSEZ	Focus	Location
1	Bostan Industrial Zone	Industry based on agricultural products, ceramics, minerals, halal food	Baluchistan
2	Rashkai Economic Zone	Pharmaceutical, textile, food and beverages, steel and various industries related to engineering.	M-I Khyber Pakhtunkhwa

3	Mohmand Marble City	Marble, Lime stone	KPK
4	PSEZ Dhabeji	Services, industries based on agricultural items	Sindh
5	Port Qasim PSEZ	Automobile, electrical goods, services	Sindh
6	China PEZ	Leather, fiber glass, machinery, industry dealing with agricultural items, pharmaceutical, cosmetics, medical equipments.	M-2 Sheikhupura Punjab
7	ICT Model Industries Zone	IT industry, electrical equipment, machinery and services.	Islamabad
8	Mirpur Industrial Zone	Fruit and Vegetable processing, edible oil industry, food processing and packaging.	Azad Jammu and Kashmir

| 9 | Moqpondass PSEZ | Precious stones processing, jewelry, fruit processing etc. | Gilgit-Baltistan (GB) |

Table of PSEZ under CPEC

Source: Special Economic Zones in Pakistan: Promises and Perils there was little progress in restoring investor confidence. Tales of corruption and terrorism in the country further vitiated the environment, making new investments less likely.[13]

After Pakistan launched series of battles to defeat foreign sponsored terrorism in the country, security environment improved. China and Pakistan believed that time was ripe for them to launch CPEC. Under the frame-work of this agreement signed in 2015 the focus is on infrastructure development. It is evident that without modern infrastructure SEZs cannot yield positive results. CPEC has four major dimensions i.e development of infrastructure, promotion of industrial ventures, progress in agricultural production and multiplication of trade links at global level. For most of these goals to succeed creation of institutional linkages is required. Special Economic Zones of various types can fill the void.

Wrong policies of Zia's military regime which resulted in collaboration with US in Afghanistan made Pakistan battle ground for proxy wars. Civilian governments which followed were not stable, they were incapable of providing continuity to national policies. Musharraf's military intervention made investment climate even worse. As already mentioned, China's experience with SEZs has been very successful. There is much Pakistan can learn from China in this regard, however, lessons learnt will have to be applied carefully keeping Pakistan's specific requirements in mind. Stake holders and decision-makers in Pakistan can also learn a great deal from Pakistan's own past experiences.

The Ministry of Industries and Production (MOIP) formulated policy for the protection of large-scale industries like chemicals, fertilizers and steel. The policy is designed to encourage exports while discouraging imports.[14] A separate institution under the name of Small and Medium Enterprise Development Authority (SMEDA) was launched in 1998 (Hussain & Vaqar 2011). If FDI in small and medium industries takes place it would lead to improvement in status of women in rural areas and small towns of Pakistan.

Provincial governments under 18th amendment have acquired the right to formulate industrial policy. In 2016 Khyber Pakhtunkhwa (KP) government made laws to encourage promotion of SEZs and development of infrastructure within the frame-work of CPEC. Other provincial governments are also eager to benefit from various SEZ schemes launched under CPEC.

Karachi Export Processing Zone (KEPZ) was followed by Risalpur Export Processing Zone (REPZ) Sialkot Export Processing Zone (SEPZ) and Gujranwala Export Processing Zone (GUEPZ). An export processing zone for Gwadar is in the final stages of planning. China has shown interest in investing in Gwadar Export Processing Zone (GEPZ). GEPZ success would lead to creation of employment opportunities for people of Baluchistan.[15]

Several economic zones have emerged all over Pakistan, the Rashkai Economic Zone (REZ) in Mardan is believed to carry great promise. Gadoon Economic Zone (GEZ) in Gadoon Amazai, (Swabi), faced problems due to a number of factors. A major reason can be attributed to opposition of business groups who for some reason could not join GEZ.

Hathar Economic Zone (HEZ) in Hathar, Haripur is another venture whose success depends on a number of factors, which should be focus of government in the next few months. Dhabeji Special Economic Zone (DSEZ) in Sindh is counted as a rather successful zone enjoying proximity to road networks and other elements promoting connectivity. A new SEZ will be located on Sialkot-Lahore motorway. This will be prime location as both Sialkot and Lahore are major industrial cities.[16] Khairpur Special Economic Zone (KSEZ) has been established by Government of Sindh, local and foreign investors will be able to benefit from KSEZ if and when it takes off. Qatar has shown interest in investing one billion dollars in a new SEZ along the motorway in Punjab. There is also a proposal made by Qatar to invest in Baluchistan.[17]

China-Pakistan Economic Zone in Gwadar, Baluchistan is an exclusive domain for Chinese investment. On the same lines there are proposals to establish a Japanese city in Pakistan to promote exclusively Japanese investment in that region.[18] Quaid-e-Azam Business Park (QABP) caters to twelve major industries including Information Technology and Electronics. It is located on Islamabad-Lahore Motorway at Sheikhupura. It is linked to all major cities, sea ports and dry ports.[19] Bostan Industrial Zone (BIZ) in district Pishin Baluchistan also enjoys prime location. It borders Quetta being 32km away from the dry port. It enjoys a number of other advantages like having access to skilled work force.

A new zone is under construction in Faisalabad, which is a major industrial city in Punjab, Pakistan. When completed it would be the biggest industrial estate of Pakistan. It has started with a special Chinese zone. Provision will be made for reserved sections for all the countries participating in the project. Under CPEC nine new PSEZs will be launched two each in Sindh and Punjab, one each in Baluchistan, KPK, Gilgit-Baltistan, Islamabad and FATA. They are considered to be very crucial for the country and will therefore be undertaken on priority basis.[20]

As already mentioned earlier there are three areas to draw lessons from in order to improve the performance of PSEZs and all types of SEZs. The most important source is Pakistan's own experiences. Learning from ones own mistakes can ensure better performance in future. China a close ally of Pakistan holds vast experience in forming SEZs and managing them efficiently. All the nations that have established successful economic ventures have looked towards China and gained from Chinese experience in this field. Lastly, we can also learn from mistakes made by other states. SEZs have not been successful in some parts of the world. These failed ventures also carry valuable lessons for states planning to establish SEZs in the future. However, there is a world of difference between learning from and copying. There is need to realize that each country has to cater to its own special conditions while learning from other countries. Blind replication of foreign ideas will not lead to positive results unless they are fine tuned in accordance with specific conditions prevailing in the country.

One important point to emerge from a study of SEZs is the primacy enjoyed by location. The decision regarding location of a SEZ should take into account availability of infrastructure like road networks, railways, air and seaports along with other means like water, electricity and connectivity with global markets. Another factor to keep under consideration is availability of raw materials for industry. If food processing industry is the main feature of the venture then, a rural location might be better, providing other factors like infrastructure are available. If machinery is to be produced it will be more economical if it is close to areas where metals are extracted and refined. If metals are imported then the SEZ would be better off if it is close to a port cum refining centre. Information technology industry should be close to population centres equipped with sound educational and research centres. Skill development centres and think tanks related to specific industry could also play a crucial role in the success of a venture. Shenzen SEZ stands out as a successful venture, in this case location is considered to have been a crucial factor. Another good example in this regard is Chittagong.[21]

Business environment and conducive culture are also important. A number of institutions have emerged in the last few years which measure traits like 'Ease of Doing Business'. The performance of each state is measured according to pre- determined criteria. An average on the basis of these criteria determines the suitability of a country. Issues like business regulations, approach of bureaucracy, provision of 'one-window-operation' and business environment are determining factors. Efficiency and mindset of staff also contribute to a higher grade on the scale of 'Ease of Doing Business'.[22] Continuity of policies and incentives is also crucial to the success of SEZs of all categories including EPZ. Pakistan moved up several notches in this realm but there is need to further improve national performance.

Demographic factors like proportion of younger element in the population can be a plus point depending on their education, technical skills and health standards. An unhealthy population could lead to absence from work, resulting in loss of working hours. Similarly illiteracy or inadequate skills can reduce production leading to higher costs of production per unit.[23] Law and order situation is vitally linked to success of SEZs. In the past poor law and order situation due to Indian sponsored terrorism and a combination of other factors resulted in flight of capital and closure of factories. SEZs performance was also affected. Political stability is also of essence as it can contribute to continuity of suitable economic policies.

As a matter of fact, there is direct linkage between law-and-order situation and political stability of the country. If one deteriorates the other cannot remain unaffected. A positive image of the country is an essential requirement for attracting FDI. In this context Pakistan's case appears to be worthy of attention. During 1980s and then again in the era of 2000, Pakistan due to wrong policies of governments in power at the time, became battle ground for various powers. India exploited the situation and started funding various terrorist groups all along Pakistan's length and breadth. Chahbahar port built by India in Iran became a centre for destabilizing Pakistan. A serving Indian naval officer working for RAW who was responsible for deaths of civilians in Pakistan was caught red handed on 3rd March 2016.

As if this was not enough India launched a propaganda war against Pakistan. It was finally discovered by European Union authorities in 2020. The epicenter of these activities was in India but many European sites were used by RAW. India fed propaganda stuff from various sites, which was then picked up by some Western sources. The fraud came to light when Indian propaganda machinery used the name of a long dead European professor. This episode led to investigations undertaken by relevant EU institutions. The revelation came as a shock. The scam is known as Dis-Info Lab run by India to malign Pakistan in the eyes of Western audience.[24]

Now that Indian cover in this case has been blown it does not mean that all is well now. The US government under Bush put pressure on Pakistan to join its so-called war on terror. But when it led to alienation of several groups Western media highlighted the situation leading to devastating consequences for the economy of Pakistan. The daunting task now confronting Pakistan is to improve its image at global level. The challenge needs to be taken up seriously and now that Dis-Info Lab run by India stands exposed there may be respite for a short period.

For successful SEZ ventures financial incentives are often considered to be important. It needs to be remembered though that in the absence of infrastructure like cheap and regular supply of electricity, even tax holidays etc will not serve any purpose. Financial incentives will make sense to investors only if accompanied by suitable policies, proper infrastructure and positive image of the country. The non-financial incentives in the form of availability of infrastructure, cheap raw materials etc may be as crucial as financial incentives to the success of SEZs.

In the case of Pakistan, the goal of increasing exports (particularly diversification of exports), increase in foreign exchange earnings etc are given significance. However, import substitution is equally important. The size of domestic market can be a plus point in this regard. While formulating policy for development and promotion of SEZs focus can be on reducing dependence on imports. This might require long process of negotiations particularly if countries investing in SEZs are exporting manufactured or semi-manufactured goods to Pakistan.

Another point to ponder while formulating SEZ policy should be utilization of natural resources available domestically. Priority should be given to industry which would use natural resources available in the country. This would suit the investors, foreign as well as domestic, as the manufacturing costs can be reduced due to comparative advantage in a particular field.

Some successful industrial clusters exist in Pakistan. The sports related cluster and surgical goods in Sialkot have functioned effectively leading to good results. The Faisalabad Textile industries cluster is also well known in Pakistan and abroad. It would be worthwhile to promote other clusters in order to speed up the process of industrialisation.[25]

To conclude it should be realised that Pakistan had export processing zone and other categories of SEZs even prior to the launching of CPEC. Some SEZs are specific to the performance of a certain function while others are designed to perform a variety of functions. A number of ventures are industrial in nature major focus being export promotion. Apart from these providing services like banking, training of human power and research-oriented activities are the focus of other ventures. Media plays quite an important role in determining success or failure of almost every economic and political endeavor. Since SEZs are no exception, they are susceptible to all kinds of pressures.

One dimension of this could be the goal of a national government to bridge the gap between developed and under-developed parts of the country. In this context the SEZs are simply viewed as a mechanism to bridge this gap. For investors profit is the most potent driving force which provides main rationale for the investment. In all such cases the goal should be finding common ground, which though difficult may not be impossible.

Pakistan should develop a team of effective negotiators. Negotiations are not about trying to impose ones point of view on the other side, but rather trying to find a solution readily acceptable to all sides. Special Economic Zones open the doors for experimentation and reform, but they should not be seen as solutions for all types of development related problems. While solving some problems they create new challenges. Effort should be made not to use good fertile soil for industrial ventures. By avoiding the use of agricultural land for industrial development one can escape the threat of food insecurity. SEZs and other industrial ventures should also avoid doing undue damage to environment. Pollution leads to health hazards and food insecurity. Fortunately, it is possible now to protect the environment while promoting economic development. For this to happen we need balanced approach so that maximum benefits are available with minimum cost.

Chapter V

1   World Investment Report 2019 UNCTAD P. 1
2   M. M. Zia, Shuja Waqar and Beenash A. Malik, 'Special Economic Zones (SEZs): A Comprehensive Analysis for CPEC SEZs in Pakistan', *The Pakistan Journal of Social Issues*, Special Issue (June 2018).
3   In Africa and parts of Asia mainly due to absence of infrastructure and lack of political stability the success rate of SEZs is lower. Lack of data also makes analysis difficult. Douglas Zhihua Zeng 'Global Experience with Special Economic Zones-With a Focus on China and Africa', *The World Bank Trade and Competitiveness Global Practice* February 2015, P9.
4   When China established SEZs the investors were offered long term lease with possibility of renewal. Due to success of this approach many other states now follow the same practice.
5   My interview with Mr Niaz Ahmed (businessman) This system has actually been applied in a few cases in Pakistan
6   Special Economic Zones in the OIC Region: Learning from Experience COMCEC Coordination Office, October 2017.
7   Zeng. Opcit P3
8   A study of history of SEZs in Central Asian states brings out main features. Land locked nature of these states was a major draw back in the past but with BRI and CPEC this problem has been resolved. See What Hinders the Development of Free Economic Zones in Kyrgyzstan? Central Asian Bureau for Analytical Reporting. https://cabar.asia/en/what-hinders-development-of-free-economic-zones-in-kyrgyzstan/
9   SEZ was setup in kandla more than fifty years ago

but it is not considered among successful ventures. According to businessmen interviewed by Matt Kennard some concessions were given to investors but now similar concessions are available to investors out of the zone https://pulitzercentre.org

10 France charges 14 of its African ex-colonies a special tax for 'building' infrastructure during colonial era. They also have to keep 50% of their foreign reserves in the French treasury. However, the state of infrastructure is so poor that SEZs have failed to take off. https://afritechnews.com Also see What is the French colonial Tax? https://afritchnews.com/french-coonial-tax

11 Iftikhar Ahmed and Zhou Taidong, 'Special Economic Zones in Pakistan: Promises and Perils', PIDE Research Report Series 2020, pp 12-13

12 Ibid.

13 Wrong policies of Zia and particularly Musharaf's attempt to support US aggression against Afghanistan caused a blowback In Pakistan in the form of terrorism

14 Iftikhar and Taidong Opcit P21.

15 Dr Ahsan Abbas and Saira Ali, Nine Proposed Priority SEZs under CPEC and SEZ Act An Approach to Industrial Development, Publication of Centre of Excellence for CPEC, Islamabad Issue 1 2018, Working paper 016, p8.

16 Ibid p 12.

17 Ibid P 14

18 Ibid P 12

19 https://www.globalvillagespace.com

20 Ahsen Abbas and Saira Ali, Opcit p 12.

21 Abbas and Ali, p 10.

22 Ease of Doing Business includes several features some of which have been innumerated above. Global Competitiveness Index also rates nations

according to Criteria set by them. https://
reports.weforum.org/global-cp,[etotovemess-
index-2017-2018/countryeconomy-profiles/
economy=pakistan

23 I was part of IBA's team working on 'Vision 2030'.
Dr Toshio Fujita was also part of the team. He was of
the view that at times due to lack of ability of some
workers to read instructions wastage can increase
leading to higher cost of production per unit.

24 According to a report presented by the
European team investigating the issue the Indian
disinformation operation continued for fifteen
years. The report further mentioned that the main
goal was to malign Pakistan and some EU and UN
related groups. https://www.disinfo.eu   Alsosee
www.dawn.com

25 Babur W. Arif and Tetsushi Sonobe, Virtual
Incubation in Industrial Clusters: A Case Study
in Pakistan March 2012 Journal of Development
Studies 48 (3):377-392. https://www.researchgate.
net/publication/254244086

Gwadar: Emerging Economic Nerve Centre of Pakistan

The establishment of Gwadar in the twenty first century is a momentous development, which is expected to shape the destiny of Pakistan and many other states of the world. It lies at the confluence of South Asia and West Asia. Its strategic value is further enhanced, as it can connect the two regions with Central Asia, which is a land locked region. If the three regions improve their infrastructure and develop connectivity all will gain from access to Gwadar deep sea port.

Gwadar is a combination of two Baluchi words, Gwa wind or air and dar door passage or route. Gwadar is therefore seen as route of wind. It enjoys many advantages over other regional ports; to begin with it is a natural deep sea port which has the capacity to handle bigger ships. It watches over Sea Lanes of Communication (SLOCs) in the Persian Gulf and Arabian Sea, which makes it possible for Pakistan to protect the Sea Lanes thereby adding to the security of its own trade routes. Another advantage is that unlike Dubai and other regional ports, it is not inside the Strait of Hormuz, which is viewed by strategists as a bottle neck. Being close to but outside the Strait of Hormuz it is not constrained by the confines of the Strait. A number of regional ports lack land connectivity, but in this sense also Gwadar appears to be better off. It is connected to West Asia, Central Asia, South Asia and China. The distance between Karachi and Gwadar via makran Coastal Highway is 622 km and 10 meters (386.5 miles) Travel time is a little over seven hours[1]. The distance between Gwadar and Chahbahar is 196.5 km via Makran coastal Highway[2].

Salman Rashid describes Gwadar as sitting on a "narrow isthmus between an arid mainland in the north and a rocky headland in the South"[3]. As already mentioned, Gwadar is a hammer shaped peninsula having two naturally curved semicircular Bays on either side. West Bay is known by the name of Paddi Zirr and East Bay is called Deymi Zirr. Its location at the 'apex of the Arabia Sea and at the mouth of Persian Gulf' adds to its strategic significance. [4]

Gwadar lies on Makran coast, it is believed to have been occupied by Bronze Age people about whom little information is available. Later it became part of Achaemenid (Persian) Empire. Cyrus the Great is believed to have conquered the region to make it part of Persian Empire. History tells us that when Alexander the Great had to return back home his admiral Nearchus, mentioned Makran in his account of the naval expedition as 'dry and mountainous inhabited by fish eaters'. Persian historians also noted this point calling the people 'Mahikhoran' or fish eaters. Perhaps the term was transformed to present day Makran over a period of several centuries.

After the collapse of Alexander's empire the region frequently changed hands. In 644 AD Muslim Arab army operating from Persia, conquered parts of Makran, but the second Caliph Hazrat Umer issued orders not to proceed further. However, in 711 AD Muslim army under the command of Muhammad bin Qasim, took control of Gwadar, making it a part of the emerging Muslim empire in South Asia. For several centuries Mughals and Safavids tried to compete for control of the region[5].

The Portuguese captured and ransacked Gwadar in late sixteenth century in keeping with worst traditions of European colonial powers. They were interested in expanding their control over resource rich parts of Asia and Africa. Makran coastline and Gwadar were seen as secure bases to achieve that goal. Resistance offered by local people resulted in the ransacking of Gwadar by the Portuguese[6]. In 1550s Ottoman Admiral Seydi Ali Reis visited Gwadar. In his memoir 'Mirat ul Mumalik' meaning the 'Mirror of Countries' he mentioned that Gwadar was inhabited by Baluch tribes and the chief was Malik jelaluddin son of Malik Dinar[7].

In the Eighteenth-Century dynastic rivalry for the control of Muscat Oman, took serious turn the contestants being Yarubi and Al Bu Saidi tribes. Sultan bin Ahmed Al Bu Saidi had to flee to Gwadar in 1783, from there he went to Kharan on his way to meet Naseer Khan 1, the powerful ruler of Kalat to seek his help. The ruler of Kalat expressed his inability to do much. However, in keeping with best traditions of Baluch hospitality and generosity he offered the refugee prince hospitality and safety. He was allowed to stay in Gwadar furthermore Gwadar's revenues were allocated to the fugitive prince for his and his family's maintenance. The idea behind the move was to help a friend in need but it was supposed to be a temporary measure. Ultimately the matter was settled between the ruling family of Oman, but after the fugitive prince got back his throne, he continued to hold on to Gwadar[8].

There is no documentary evidence to suggest that Gwadar was permanently handed over to Oman. The ruler after being restored to his throne simply did not return Gwadar back to its rightful owner the ruler of Kalat.

Some accounts suggest that Gwadar was part of dowry given by ruler of Kalat to his daughter, at the time of her marriage to the son of the ruler of Oman. Again there is no documentary evidence of this transaction having taken place either. What we do know is that Oman continued to hold on to Gwadar for more than one hundred and seventy five years. During this period the people of Gwadar and other parts of Makran had the option of serving in Oman army and police force. The services they rendered provided the families with a dependable source of sustenance. Travel between Oman and Gwadar was easy and people moved around freely in the region.

Those who know Gwadar well say that even to this day the cultural impact of interaction with Oman is quite evident. Religious affinity which was already in existence, coupled with geographical proximity, provided better chances of assimilation. Arab cultural impact is reflected in cuisine and the way people dress up, and of course majority of people were bilingual having recourse to both Arabic and Baluchi. When the British occupied the South Asian subcontinent in 1857, they accepted the status quo. The main focus of their policy was to establish control over the Persian Gulf and to bring the entire region under their sovereignty.

They left no stone unturned towards achieving this objective, and ultimately succeeded in achieving their goals. The British colonial administration conducted a survey in 1861 for the purpose of laying a telegraph line along the Makran coast. They were impressed by the location of Gwadar midway between Karachi Port and Bandar Abbas. They looked upon Gwadar as an ideal location to serve as main headquarters, for the effective management of the telegraph network, connecting them to England and rest of the world[9].

When Pakistan became independent in 1947 it was beset with many problems, like the settlement of millions of refugees migrating from India. Moreover, India launched war against Pakistan to occupy Kashmir in 1948. India also stopped the supply of river waters to Pakistan; In Pakistan it was seen as an attempt to destroy Pakistan's agriculture, destabilize its economy and undermine its food security.

While all this was going on princely states like Bahawalpur, Kalat and others started joining Pakistan. There was a movement in Gwadar launched by people who wanted to join Pakistan. The strategic importance of Gwadar and Makran coast was also evident to Pakistani strategists.

A few years after independence while the Indian pressure was still there, Pakistan's civilian leadership started preparing long term development plans for the country. Gwadar was seen as a great asset for the future. Negotiations with Oman were undertaken in 1954, they were proceeding at slow pace. Actually 'great game' for the control of Gwadar had begun. India with the tacit approval of some powerful elements in the British government tried to acquire control over Gwadar. It would have been no less than a political catastrophe had India acquired control over such a strategic asset of Pakistan. On the other hand the US was encouraging the Shah of Iran to also lay his claim to Gwadar. Although the cases of India and Iran were legally on weak grounds, but they enjoyed the support of strong states.

Pakistan was lucky to have a visionary figure as Prime Minister, Malik Feroz Khan Noon, and his wife Begum Viqarunnisa Noon, regarded the challenge to be serious and devised a realistic strategy to acquire Gwadar for Pakistan.[10] The lady reached UK in 1956 and launched an effective lobbying campaign in favour of Pakistan's case regarding Gwadar. Her efforts were successful and finally the British parliament passed a resolution in Pakistan's favour[11]. The details are given in Malik Noon's memoirs *From Memory*; He remained Pakistan's Prime Minister from 16 December 1957 to October 1958, but during this short period of ten months he accomplished a great deal.

Salman Rashid in his book *Gwadar Song of the Sea Wind* has acknowledged the role of Mr Noon, but he has projected a different perspective regarding Begum Noon from the one generally proclaimed by historians. Gwadar's transfer to Pakistan took four years after the beginning of negotiations. The transfer documents were ready during Mr Noon's premiership but the ruler of Oman wanted 3 million dollars for handing over Gwadar to Pakistan. Pakistan did not have the sum demanded by Oman. At this point Aga Khan the spiritual leader of Ismaili community stepped in to help Pakistan gain full sovereignty over the deep sea port[12]. On 8 December 1958 Pakistan was able to incorporate Gwadar formally into the newly established state[13].

The strategic value of regions vary according to technological developments, discovery of natural resources and changes in political and strategic environment. Gwadar's strategic significance was enhanced due to a combination of factors. It was always a deep sea port, but that factor began to go in its favour, when huge ships were introduced and deep sea ports became a great asset. As already stated earlier, its connectivity to resource rich areas and proximity to states, which are dependent on these resources has further increased its importance. One weak link in this emerging scenario was absence of infrastructure, now with the launching of BRI this gap is being gradually filled. When the region becomes well connected Gwadar will promote regional peace and prosperity.

According to Mehnaz Ispahani, Soviet Union was interested in acquiring access to Gwadar and other ports on Makran coast[14]. This would have bestowed two clear advantages on Soviet Union. The role of Soviet navy in the Indian Ocean would have received a boost, enabling it to tackle the activities of hostile Western navies, which were already well entrenched in the Indian Ocean region. Another major advantage would be that Soviet controlled resource rich Central Asian territories would get direct access to their foreign markets. In 1969 Soviets asked Pakistan for permission to build highway from Chaman towards Gwadar, Pasni, Ormara, Jivani or Somiani[15]. It was also reported that the Soviets were interested in constructing a road to Karachi linking it with Afghanistan.

Soviet interest in the small coastal cities in Baluchistan was noted with concern by some people in Pakistan[16]. The Khan of Kalat is reported to have expressed his concern regarding Soviet interest in Gwadar. He believed this to be a serious threat to Pakistan's security[17]. However, Pakistan rejected all the Soviet proposals in this regard, due to Soviet Union's close relations with India, and its perceived animosity towards China.

US Admiral Thomas Moorer called for establishment of a US naval base in Gwadar in 1980[18]. Since this proposal came in the aftermath of Soviet intervention in Afghanistan, one can interpret this development as US response to Soviet challenge. Admiral Moorer like some other Western strategists believed that, Soviet rationale for being in Afghanistan was to take control of Gwadar. To preempt this move he wanted to see US naval fleet stationed at Gwadar. Although US had access to several ports in the Persian Gulf which had been developed into naval bases, establishing another base at a strategic location could give additional advantage.

According to Andrew Small, Mr Zulfiqar Ali Bhutto in late 1970s, offered US the opportunity to build Gwadar port, but the US did not avail the offer. This account appears to be superficial, as there is no mention of conditions to be fulfilled by the US, prior to the takeover. Even the year when the offer was made has not been precisely stated. Neither has a reason been mentioned as to why US administration declined the offer.

On the other hand, Ispahani has mentioned that Mr Z.A. Bhutto offered the US use of Gwadar, in 1973-74 in return for lifting the arms embargo imposed by US against Pakistan[19]. The US was probably under the impression that by refusing to cooperate, they will be able to stall the development of Gwadar as a port. Their interest in Pakistan had also declined considerably after Pakistan tried to pursue an independent foreign policy.

Pakistan chalked out plans for developing Gwadar as a port in 1958, soon after acquiring control over the port. In 1960s and even later the plans were drawn and refined, but nothing could be done due to paucity of financial resources. The task of building Gwadar port was therefore left for a later era. It was realized by Pakistani strategists that Karachi port would be vulnerable during conditions of war. Their worst fears turned out to be correct when India tried to blockade Karachi in 1971 and again during the Kargil crisis[20].

The fact that Peoples Republic of China emerged as a major economic power, with plans to develop Xinjiang autonomous region, as a new industrial hub worked in Pakistan's favour. Pakistan's plans to focus on economic development of Baluchistan coincided with Chinese policy of developing Xinjiang and other regions of China.

It was decided to develop Gwadar as the only deep sea port of Pakistan with assistance from China. Pakistan and China decided to develop CPEC in November 2014. Pakistan wanted to fully benefit from this opportunity.[21] China was looking for a shorter route to carry oil and gas from Middle East to factories in Xinjiang. Manufactured goods from Western China could also be carried to markets in Africa and Middle East through the Gwadar port.

In early part of twenty first century the prospects of Gwadar improved. Blue prints had already been in existence, the task of building the port was given to a Chinese company. Phase one started in 2002 and took five years to complete, 2007 marked the end of phase one. During this period roads, bridges and highways were built. The physical infrastructure had been lacking before 2002. The second phase was launched in 2007 and took six years to complete. During the second phase building the port facilities were the main focus of both governments.

Development of Gwadar and Other Parts of Makran Coast

Makran Coastal Highway was constructed with Chinese cooperation, it is a modern highway which has connected Gwadar and other cities like Pasni, Ormara, Jivani and Somiani with Karachi and other parts of Sindh. Makran Coastal Highway has reduced travel time by several hours. Gwadar and other coastal towns are connected to Northern parts of Pakistan, through the North-South connecting highways ultimately linking Gwadar with Karakoram Highway, and through it to Xinjiang. Ormara has been developed as a naval base by Pakistan Navy. It will provide protection to sea lanes of commercial and strategic importance, along with the responsibility of protecting CPEC maritime trade routes.

According to Nadir Mir the Master Plan for development of Makran coast is elaborate. Under it Jivani will be developed as a centre of tourism, bringing a lot of investment which will open up economic opportunities for local people. The sunset at Jivani enjoys a lot of fame within the country and abroad. Jivani's potential as a tourist spot attracted attention of planners after CPEC was launched[22]. Pasni is being developed as a fishing port with modern facilities for fish processing and storage. Local fishermen should be helped to acquire modern fishing trawlers in order to compete with others fishing in the area. An industrial zone in Pasni is also being planned. Somiani already has a

Space Research Centre run by SUPARCO[23], among new plans a natural park, aquarium and other facilities are being envisaged. There are some armed forces facilities already located at Somiani. The infrastructure has improved in the last few years. Among other important CPEC related plans is a transit highway to Central Asian republics[24.]

The task of drawing a master plan for Gwadar was far more elaborate, having two clear dimensions. The relationship between Gwadar port and Gwadar city is symbiotic. Their roles are interlinked and they reinforce each other; having said this, one needs to bear in mind that the two have been designed to perform specific functions. Several drafts of the master plan had to be formulated, each carrying a different price tag.

The seventy five page final document emerged after hectic efforts made by China Communications Construction Company, Pakistan's Ministry of Planning and Development and Gwadar Development Authority. It provides an elaborate road map of how Gwadar is to emerge as a trade and economic hub, of the region in the next couple of decades.

The document has been renamed 'Gwadar Smart City Master Plan' under which Gwadar's economy will surpass $30bn per annum. In the long term the per capita income in Gwadar has been calculated to be in the range of $15000 per annum, which will be much higher than the average per capita income in other parts of Pakistan. Gwadar is expected to become the third largest city of Pakistan in terms of economic output.

Six special features of the plan stand out: a) high-tech industries will be encouraged by the government in order to enhance the level of economic development. b) Highly paid jobs will encourage people with suitable qualifications to move towards these centers. It will also motivate Baluch youth to equip themselves with latest knowledge. c) A lot of activity in construction sector will take place as housing, educational centres, health facilities, mega shopping malls and luxury resorts will be developed. d) Gwadar will have Pakistan's largest international airport. This is considered to be an essential requirement in view of Gwadar's emerging role as a regional economic and tourism hub. e) The economic planners have introduced the idea of developing some man-made islands the purpose of which is not very clear. f) In order to attract investment for various grand projects tax-free environment is envisaged[25].

One problem being experienced by the people of Gwadar and other cities of Pakistan is uncertain supply of electricity. A five billion dollar investment was made in the power sector, with fifteen new power plants, to resolve the problem of electricity disruptions. One billion dollars were invested into generating 700,000 m3 of fresh water per day through desalination plants.

Ambitious plans for expansion of educational facilities have also been chalked out. University of Turbat established its regional campus at Gwadar in 2016. Academic activities started in January 2017. Four BS programmes were launched in the field of Computer Science (BSIT) Management Sciences (BBA) Commerce (BS commerce) and Education (B.Ed.).

Centres of Excellence are being established with Chinese support. Local students are interested in learning Chinese language and culture. China Study Centres and Confucius Centres are already operating in many universities of Pakistan. Other major areas of interest for students in Baluchistan can be information technology, medical sciences, and energy related branches of engineering, desalination technology, dam construction, agriculture, animal husbandry and poultry farming. Some of these degree courses have already been launched but much remains to be done[26].

The government came up with the plan to establish University of Gwadar in 2017. Land was allocated for the purpose and funds were also provided. Faculty was hired keeping merit as the main criterion but preference was to be given to candidates from Baluchistan. It generated a lot of interest in civil society. People were happy that their sons and daughters will be able to acquire quality education within their own city. It is expensive and beyond the means of less affluent parents to send their wards to other cities for education. Besides economic factors cultural aspects need to be taken into account. In my interviews with parents of young girls, it transpired that the doors of higher education are closed for most young girls, due to absence of higher education facilities within the city.

Mariyam Suleman a freelance writer from Gwadar has analysed some of the factors which have resulted in slow pace of development. According to her prospects for establishment of University of Gwadar became bright when government announced development package for Gwadar in May 2017. It included 300-bed hospital, desalination plant and a University[27]. Under CPEC there is a plan to identify willing Chinese universities for collaboration with Pakistani universities in areas of mutual interest. Slow pace of implementation of plans is a major problem. I personally attribute this to two factors. Firstly, when a government initiates a programme the next government instead of promoting it tries to launch its own plans. Secondly, bureaucratic approach could be an additional draw back.

Mariyam Suleman interviewed Nasir Rahim Sohrabi an academician who heads Rural Community Development Council (RCDC). According to him educational institutions which exist offer very few disciplines; many students still have to travel to cities like Quetta, Karachi or Lahore for acquiring higher education in disciplines which are not being offered in Gwadar. The delay in establishing University of Gwadar is also being attributed to paucity of funds, which the government has not been able to allocate. Many young faculty members have proceeded abroad to acquire higher education. The majority of these young people will be pursuing their education in Chinese Universities.

National University of Modern Languages (NUML) has opened a campus in Gwadar. The idea is to equip the Baluch youth with knowledge of Chinese and other modern languages. A knowledge corridor is emerging under CPEC and in my opinion Gwadar is well placed to benefit from this development. The Pakistan Navy has established cadet colleges in the coastal areas to provide good quality education to young people of the region. Pakistan Army has also established cadet colleges in other parts of Baluchistan.

The UN ESCAP Committee on Science and Technology and Innovation Chairman Dr Atta-ur-Rahman served as former Chairman of HEC. In one of his articles he suggested that Pakistan should focus on its economy, transforming it from low-value to a higher value-added knowledge economy. According to him such transformation can occur only if CPEC becomes a 'knowledge corridor'. Gwadar should be more than a port carrying Chinese goods to other countries[28]. Many other scholars who are visionaries, see Gwadar and other cities of Pakistan as future centers of knowledge, opening the way for Pakistan's economic and intellectual progress[29].

Under Gwadar Master Plan the total area allocated for the city is 1201.15 sq km out of which 310.62 sq km will be reserved for development purposes, 64.52 sq km for the establishment of industrial area, 4.67 sq km for establishment of warehouses and logistics facilities. A Free Zone will be established at Gwadar under which 13.19 sq km has been proposed for Gwadar Oil City.

A Special Economic Zone with a number of projects will also be launched. Other sectors for which land has been allocated are road and infrastructure development, business and commercial ventures, administrative facilities, housing, defense, transport, recreation and entertainment. An area of 11.69 sq km has been reserved for creation of municipal utilities.

Apart from developmental projects drawn for Gwadar city, special projects were planned for Gwadar Port area. After Port Authority of Singapore (PAS) failed to develop Gwadar Port it was handed over to China Overseas Port Holding Company (COPHC). Musharraf government's decision to hand over Gwadar Port to PAS in 2007 was an unwise decision. It was argued by some that there was a lot of Western pressure on Musharraf, but the fact that he succumbed to this pressure does not speak well of him as a 'leader '. An agreement was signed in February 2007 for handing over of

Gwadar Port to PSA for forty-year period. PSA was given the task to further develop and operate the port. Five hundred and eighty four acres of land was to be developed as Special Economic Zone. According to some accounts PSA felt constrained as the land marked for SEZ could not be handed over to it due to opposition from Pakistan Navy on grounds of security.

Another reason often mentioned is that foreign sponsored terrorist group's scared away potential investors including PSA. Perhaps the most cogent factor was the opposition from some Western countries, who wanted to see Gwadar fail as a venture or at least to delay its emergence as much as possible. In 2013 as a result of mutual agreement PSA and Pakistan decided to terminate the agreement.

In the same year COPHC entered into a forty-year agreement to further develop and run the port. The six year period from 2007 to 2013 did not see much progress as far as development of infrastructure and other facilities were concerned. However, since 2013 much work has been done and the port is now fully operational, ships have started arriving. COPHC invested $300 million, all the four multipurpose berths are fully operational now[30]. By 2030 the number of berths will further increase. Under the long-term vision by 2045 the number of berths will be increased to hundred[31]. A liquified Natural gas terminal will also be established soon.

Work has started in full swing on a desalination plant to convert five million gallons of seawater into drinking water. A 300 megawatts coal-fired power plant has also been established, it will be fully functional by 2023, according to Gwadar Development Authority Director General Shahzeb Khan Kakar[32].

Mr Zhang Baozhong the Chairman of COPHC in his interview with Express Tribune, maintained that the impression that CPEC has slowed down is not correct. According to him many CPEC projects have been completed ahead of time in spite of the Pandemic. Talking about the future of Gwadar he said that as a result of CPEC, Gwadar will emerge as the largest port in the region, besides being a significant global economic hub[33]. The Express Tribune report also stated that forty three Chinese firms were all set to invest in Gwadar's Special Economic Zone. In addition to these, two hundred other Chinese firms have also been registered.

Gwadar Port and Gwadar Free Zone (GFZ) are expected to generate $10bn per annum besides creating thousands of jobs. Till June 2021 67,000 tons of cargo had been handled at Gwadar Port. Consignments under Afghan Transit Trade Agreement, were handled by the port and then transported to Afghanistan.

In the first phase GFZ would be spread over 60 acres of land with forty seven registered enterprises. Six factories have been completed and six more are under construction. The second phase of GFZ would be spread over 2,221 acres of land. COPHC has already lined up an investor to launch the second phase of GFZ, which would require additional 1600 acres of land. The $3 billion investment in single industry would create 30,000 jobs[34].

Under the Belt and Road Initiative China has decided to build 'Digital Silk Road' in Pakistan linking it to Africa and Europe. This would serve geostrategic interests of China, Pakistan and other member states of BRI. The connectivity will be through a submarine cable in the Arabian Sea. At present international telecommunication consortium, dominated by Western and Indian companies operates the system. China is interested in promoting the development of physical infrastructure but major focus appears to be on digital projects.

The Hengtong Group of China is a leading fiber optic and power cable making group. It heads the consortium of telecommunication companies. Pakistan, East Africa and other regions will be connected to Europe (PEACE) cable in the Indian Ocean and Mediterranean region. Work has started and laying of sea cable in Pakistan's territorial waters began in March 2021. For this purpose, an Arabian Sea landing station has been constructed in Karachi, by Cabernet a local company, providing internet services. In the Mediterranean region a cable has already been laid from Egypt to France. The 15,000 km long cable was expected to be ready by December 2021.

The Special Communication Organisation, the telecommunications branch of Pakistan Army, is ready to lay a fiber optic cable, connecting Rawalpindi with Karachi and Gwadar. The project is estimated to cost $240 million, it is in collaboration with China's Huawei Technologies. The system will be connected to PEACE cable. The fiber optic cable links the Xinjiang region in Southwest China to Rawalpindi, where Pakistan Army headquarter is also located. The idea is to further secure the communication link between China and Pakistan[35].

The emergence of Gwadar as a major economic centre depends on several factors, one of which is existence of high quality communication infrastructure. The PEACE cable for the first time in the history of Gwadar, will provide it with fiber optic connectivity, to all major cities of Pakistan and beyond. Through the PEACE cable Pakistan's dependence on India will be reduced, which is essential in view of sensitive nature of information, and India's hostility towards Pakistan and China.[36]

Emerging Challenges and Their Solutions

The promotion of education, development of connectivity projects and technological upgradation, will lead to interaction between people and, enhance pace of economic progress. The combination of all these factors could pave the way for changes in future. Status quo oriented groups are generally opposed to change and view the process with suspicion. There is also a risk that emerging challenges, if not properly managed could also lead to manipulation, by various internal and external forces.

The population of Gwadar is expected to register tremendous increase in the next few decades. Preference will be given to people of Gwadar and other parts of Baluchistan, however, in technical fields in the absence of local expertise, qualified people from other parts of Pakistan and abroad will have to be given a chance. Special rules and regulations in keeping with local people's sensitivities, can be formulated. But the strategy should be to keep a balance between progress and demographic balance. Access to education and interaction with different cultural groups could lead to cultural changes. People often try to resist change without realising that change cannot be prevented, it can only be managed. A complicating factor in the present scenario is involvement of external forces, which have tried to exploit local grievances to their own advantage.

There are issues like shortage of clean drinking water, electricity outages, lack of health and educational facilities, poverty etc. As already pointed out Pakistan on its own, and in collaboration with China, has taken practical steps to deal with these challenges. Desalination plants are being put up to meet water needs of the population. Similarly, power plants using coal, oil/gas and non-traditional sources of energy, are being established to provide abundant, and cheap electricity to people as well as industry[37].

The President of Peoples Republic of China has gifted a hospital to the people of Gwadar. The government of Pakistan in May 2017 announced the establishment of a hospital in Gwadar. This is just the beginning, much more will have to be done in order to remove public grievances. The armed forces have thrown open the doors of their educational and medical institutions for the people of Baluchistan. Education is the foundation of nation building exercise, its significance can be denied at nation's own peril. The federal and provincial governments need to coordinate their strategies to deal with this national challenge. Slow pace of work, inefficient implementation, lack of coordination between various departments and, scarcity of resources are some of the hurdles facing the projects.

In order to link Gwadar Port with the city and rest of the country Eastbay Expressway had to be constructed. The fishermen had been using that track of land to gain access to the sea, they fear that after the construction of the road, they would be cut off from their main source of livelihood. To redress the problem the government started work on construction of three bridges[38]. The government of Baluchistan was happy, that for launching the Eastbay Expressway project, no section of population was displaced. The happiness was short-lived as it was soon realized that people were facing other types of problems even though they were not uprooted.

However, timely action saved the situation to a large extent. In future all stake holders should be consulted in advance, but no one should have veto power to stall developmental projects. Solutions can be found with mutual agreement even before the emergence of crisis situation. Under certain circumstances people may be uprooted during implementation of developmental projects. This can lead to conflict; the only way to save the situation is to take the people into confidence and, to pay timely and adequate compensation to the affectees.

Issues of governance and administrative challenges do arise as a result of implementation of projects. Efficiency and crisis management skills are of essence. Coordination between various relevant departments carries great importance. These gigantic developmental projects have been undertaken in Pakistan in a big way since 2015. It will take time for bureaucracy and other sections of government to learn the necessary skills.

For the last several months, another crisis at the centre of which are also fishermen, has been dominating national as well as social media. The fishermen of Baluchistan want foreign fishing trawlers to be banned from the coast of Makran. They are also opposed to trawlers from Sindh from operating in the region. Big businesses from Pakistan and some foreign corporations have entered the race; they are much better equipped which is reflected in their much bigger catches of fish. The government should provide interest free loans to Makran fishermen to buy modern fishing trawlers. Needless to say they will have to be given proper training to efficiently use the equipment. Fish industry can be promoted by the government, it will be a source of revenue for the government, provide food security to the people and ensure welfare of fishermen.

Security of personnel both Pakistani and Chinese is a major issue due to hostility of anti-CPEC forces. Workers and engineers engaged in CPEC projects have been targeted by TTP and Baluch terrorist groups, financed by Indian and some other intelligence agencies. The government decided to fence areas in Gwadar in order to keep a check on people who enter sensitive areas. People carrying identity documents are facilitated by security staff. The documents are checked at points of entry and it's ensured that, those gaining entry are not in possession of arms. These measures perhaps a bit inconvenient for people at times, are essential to maintain public safety under the prevailing circumstances.

Due to the influence of political groups some sections of media have started a campaign against fencing. There is no alternative to this policy for now at least, as providing security to people is a basic responsibility of the government. People should be taken into confidence and they should be made to realize, that the security measures are temporary in nature, with improvement in security environment, there will be relaxation of security procedures. Less intrusive security measures like CCTV Cameras, gates to detect arms and other modern methods can be introduced to make security fool-proof. However, all this will be possible only after security situation registers visible improvement[39].

Another issue which has received attention of local media is the land issue. It has been suggested that land is not available for expanding Special Economic Zone in Gwadar. Gwadar Free Zone is also crucial for promoting economic development in the region. Non-availability of suitable land for promotion of development is seen as a major hurdle. Pakistan navy was allocated over 584 acres of land in Gwadar region for building naval defense related infrastructure. Due to shortage of space navy vacated 500 acres of land in 2014. It was transferred to Gwadar Port Authority (GPA) as directed by PM office, in February 2021.

The cabinet Committee on CPEC directed various ministries to take control of another 72 acres of land for various projects. However, Pakistan Navy considers the remaining land in its possession to be vital for maintaining maritime security of Gwadar and other coastal areas of Baluchistan[40]. It can hardly be denied that maritime threats to the security of Gwadar do exist, the navy is also responsible for providing security to maritime trade routes of CPEC. A solution to this problem should be found soon, keeping in view the security and developmental requirements of the country.

Importance of Gwadar for CPEC: Security Threats

The emergence of Gwadar as a geo-strategic nerve centre and economic hub, speaks volumes about the shift in balance of power. The importance of maritime and land trade routes, has been recognized by historians, many of whom still believe that politics of trade routes has been a major motivating factor behind history. A combination of geographical factors has enhanced the importance of Gwadar as a port. Besides being a deep sea port it has now been connected to China, Central Asia and Afghanistan in the north, with Middle East in the west and Africa in the south. The oil pipelines carrying oil from Middle East, feed into a network bringing oil from Central Asia and Russia, thus integrating Persian Gulf oil producing regions with Pacific Ocean and Caspian Sea region[41].

Through Gwadar China has got direct access to Indian Ocean; this connectivity will reduce the distance between China and its markets in the Middle East and Africa. It will also enable China to get oil and raw materials in less time and at a lower cost, for its industrial centres in Xinjiang. Chinese policy of focusing on economic development of Xinjiang will also get a boost.

Over the last decade China has focused on increasing its options. From being totally dependent on Strait of Malacca, it now has access to four ports in the Indian Ocean two of which i.e. Gwadar and Kyaukpyu are connected with it through land route as well.

The increase in Chinese influence in the Indian Ocean region will create a new political and military balance in the region. Western influence will not be replaced but would rather be balanced by Chinese presence in the region. This will provide some relief to regional states, which were vary of unbridled Western domination of Indian Ocean. The US is trying to strengthen Indian hold on IOR which is bound to adversely impact Pakistan. Pakistan views with favour Chinese presence in IOR.

The emerging scenario is viewed as a win-win situation by Pakistani strategists. It helps Pakistan focus on its policy of promoting economic development of Baluchistan. One of the factors promoting discontentment in Baluchistan was lack of facilities and job opportunities for people. These were serious issues and for the last several years, the federal as well as provincial governments main focus has been to address these problems. The quicker the province returns to normalcy the better for all.

With peace in the region, Pakistan hopes to become centre of trade and political cooperation. Economic integration between China, Central Asia, Afghanistan, Pakistan, Middle East and Africa would be beneficial for all. It will give rise to cooperation, remove discontentment and discord and if these dreams materialize, people of Pakistan and the region will be real beneficiaries. Their economic condition will improve and poverty alleviation will take place. Pakistan will generate revenue from Gwadar, the land routes and the oil and gas pipelines passing through Pakistani territory. This will give stability to Pakistan's economy and, we might be able to save ourself from the embarrassment, of knocking at the door of IMF. Pakistan's political clout will increase as a result of participation in this inter regional connectivity grouping.

The status quo-oriented powers including the US, several European powers, Australia and India are not happy with emerging dynamics of geo-strategic environment. The Western opposition is directed more against rising power of China, although they also want to keep Pakistan in a subservient and dependent relationship[42]. India on the other hand views China as a powerful adversary but at the same time it sees Pakistan as an enemy state. It was responsible for the breakup of Pakistan in 1971 and now, probably fears that Pakistan will settle the score as soon as it gets a chance. Now India is trying to destabilize the provinces of Baluchistan and Khyber Pakhtunkhwa, which will automatically disrupt CPEC. However, with the victory of Taliban in Afghanistan it may not be as easy to accomplish their goals as under US occupied Afghanistan.

Pakistani and Chinese strategists are focusing on assessing the nature of threats confronting CPEC. The determination of sources of threats is also important. According to strategists, US and Western powers are much less likely to enter the arena, they are more likely to use India as a proxy to achieve their objectives. A range of possibilities exist out of which three appear to be more credible. Employment of direct military threat would be a highly risky affair but it cannot be ruled out altogether. Military steps short of war have been employed in other scenarios and Pakistani strategists attach some importance to this possibility. The most credible threat being considered by strategists, under the current scenario, is hybrid warfare or fifth generation warfare.

Pakistan and India have used traditional military power against each other on three occasions i.e. 1948, 1965 and 1971. On the first two occasions the performance of Pakistani forces was impressive but in 1971 the nature of conflict was different and the outcome was disappointing. India is five times bigger than Pakistan in terms of population and the same ratio is reflected in the size of armed forces. As far as land ratio is concerned India is four times larger than Pakistan. Nuclear capability of Pakistan is an equalizer. India's numerical strength stands neutralized but nuclear capability is useful only as a deterrent. Actual use of nuclear weapons can be contemplated only under a very narrow and specific set of circumstance. Since acquiring nuclear capability, the two South Asian states have engaged in Kargil crisis which was a short and limited war.

India has been trying to surround Pakistan with states which would serve as India's military allies. US occupied Afghanistan was an asset for India. RAW and CIA sponsored terrorist groups used Afghan soil against Pakistan. Iran also developed close relations with India and allowed Chahbahar to be used as an intelligence gathering and terrorist base. However, there were no known Indian military bases in either country. Indian policy of encircling Pakistan failed particularly after the liberation of Afghanistan and change in Iranian approach under Chinese influence.

The skirmishes between regular forces of China and India in Ladakh recently reflect the inability of Indian forces to take pressure. India also fears the possibility of a two-front war, under which China and Pakistan could coordinate their military strategy. Considering all these factors, it does not appear likely, that India would use the military option even under Western pressure.

Another source of threat to regional peace could be effort on the part of either state to pursue military methods short of war. On at least two occasions Indian submarines were found in Pakistan's territorial waters; they were challenged and forced to leave. During Kargil crisis India tried to blockade the Karachi port[43]. India tried to test Pakistan's air defense capability by firing a nuclear capable missile into Pakistani territory in March 2022. The problem with this approach is that escalation cannot be ruled out of the equation. Increase in tension and step by step escalation can lead to full-fledged war.

Hybrid Warfare In post-World War II scenario a new form of warfare has been used by states against their adversaries. The concept was projected for the first time according to one account by Mockaitis in 1995. In 2006 Frank G. Hoffman colonel in US army also used the term to denote a similar notion. It has also been called by other names, which has probably added to confusion, surrounding the term. A careful reading of history suggests that this form of warfare was employed in a less complex form by states several centuries back.

If the concept occupied the minds of strategists centuries back then what is new about it? As the political system is becoming more complex so are the concepts of statehood and warfare. Hybrid warfare or fifth generation warfare is a strategy whereby traditional forms of military force may be combined with political forms, low intensity warfare, terrorism, psychological pressurization, economic sabotage and even biological warfare are used to undermine the adversary. All these forms may not be used in each and every case. Different tools are used according to the vulnerability of the adversary. The goal is always to undermine the faith of people in the government and armed forces, and to bring about economic and political collapse of the adversary.

The generation of fear psychosis, feelings of insecurity and loss of faith in ideology add to confusion. Terrorism stops the process of economic development and in combination with economic sanctions etc. common people's economic woes are aggravated. All these issues lead to political and psychological consequences. By employing political, economic and other tools the adversaries try to promote the collapse of the state or at least change of regime.

The CIA frequently used terrorism and sabotage against Communist states during the Cold War to undermine faith in government. After break up of Soviet Union 'color revolutions' have been promoted to bring about regime change in many of these states. US introduced CIA trained groups to topple the Cuban government during early 1960s.

During 1980s it was stated by some journalists that CIA trained US citizens of Chinese origin were infiltrated into China. Iraq suffered due to hybrid war tactics of CIA. A secular country was turned into a sectarian quigmire by the US agencies. More than five hundred Iraqi intellectuals were murdered under US occupation[44]. Israel used terror tactics to assassinate Iran's scholars and nuclear scientists. The list is long and shockingly, the stronger states employed hybrid warfare against the weaker ones. They could do so with impunity due to their influence over 'global media'.

Pakistan has been deeply affected by hybrid warfare ever since US and NATO presence in Afghanistan. India was given free hand by the Western powers to use Afghan soil, to promote its own goals and objectives. The US and Indian interests coincided as both wanted to scuttle CPEC. The entire route of KKH, Gilgit-Baltistan and particularly Gwadar became the target of hostile intelligence agencies.

After the liberation of Afghanistan the newly formed government seized documents from Indian consulates in areas adjacent to Pakistan. Some of these were shared with Pakistan. They clearly establish Indian funding and training of terrorist groups operating in Baluchistan and other parts of Pakistan[45].

According to Corps Commander of Baluchistan more than one dozen intelligence agencies are operating in Baluchistan[46]. For different reasons most of them are trying to sabotage Gwadar's emergence, as a regional economic and political hub. Their main target is CPEC. The Indian sponsored terrorism in Gwadar and other parts of Pakistan uses local groups like BLA, TTP, MQM (L) and other criminal groups. But for more sophisticated operations they use their own well trained military and intelligence operatives. Kulbhushan Jadhav is a living example, he was a serving Indian naval officer on deputation to RAW, operating under cover of businessman based in Chahbahar. He was handling and funding a large group of local terrorists.

The Western approach is more sophisticated; their journalists and scholars are often part of a wider network. Collection of information and occasional instigation of a certain reaction are part of the exercise. Recently in my interviews with my ex-students and Baluch and Pathan youth in general I discerned a pattern. The foreign journalists and scholars ask loaded questions like 'why do you tolerate fences?' 'Why has Chinese presence not evoked a stronger response?' 'Why is Pakistan army presence in Gwadar tolerated?'

The terrorist group's main target are Chinese citizens, Pakistani and Chinese workers engaged to work for Chinese companies, and CPEC projects. The terrorists also target infrastructure like pipelines, roads, bridges and dams. The objective is to disrupt CPEC and other projects leading to economic development and poverty alleviation. Terrorism has already had negative impact on developmental projects and, if this trend continues and poverty prevails, these same groups will use the public grievances to generate support for themselves[47].

A Pakistan army major revealed an interesting episode. According to him on Sunday morning he decided to have brunch at a place which had just been inaugurated. It was a great experience, he was able to meet some young people from University of Baluchistan. One of the students wanted to know why the presence of armed forces was necessary in Gwadar. The major told the young man 'you live in a very important, emerging hub of this region, if Pakistan army does not protect the people some foreign army will take over. That would undermine your security.' This answer is meaningful, it clearly manifests the vulnerabilities facing all regional states. There are no simple solutions. Regional states need to come out of their narrow nationalistic perspectives in order to face twenty first century challenges.

In order to fight the challenge of hybrid war in Baluchistan, only traditional military approach may not be enough. Intelligence agency's role will be crucial, it should be as non-intrusive as possible, but the goal should be promotion of efficiency, operational effectiveness and public satisfaction. Effort will have to be made to ensure, that benefits of economic development reach common people.

With better health and educational facilities, some of the public grievances will be addressed. Bringing Baluch youth to the mainstream of national life will be possible with increase in job opportunities.

Addressing foreign involvement is a 'bigger challenge' those who are involved in heinous crimes like murders and blowing up of infrastructure should receive punishment under the laws. Trial takes ages which kills the very purpose i.e. deterrence. Trials should not be protracted[48].

Many Pakistanis believe that foreign journalists and scholars should be discouraged from visiting Gwadar for their own safety. In my opinion the whetting of foreigners should be done more carefully and foreign citizens should be allowed to visit the region only after carefully checking their credentials. Currently system of 'No Objection Certificate' (NOC) is in place and, all foreigners have to acquire NOC before visiting Gwadar and other sensitive areas. This appears to be a meaningless exercise as according to Kaplan the NOC is never checked. This might tempt foreigners to visit these areas without acquiring an NOC. The present system is being run inefficiently and it has left the door wide open for foreign operatives in the garb of journalists and scholars.

If Gwadar is to really become an economic and political hub, and add to Pakistan's clout in a globalized world a lot of effort will have to be made. This dream can become a reality only if sponsors of terrorism are uprooted from the region. To quote Kaplan there have been great cities in the past, many great cities exist today and the process will continue. Gwadar can become a great city of the future.

Chapter VI

1   http://distancebetween2.com

2   https://www.prokerala.com

3   Salman Rashid *Gwadar Song of the Sea Wind*, (Lahore; Sang-e-Meel Publications, 2021) p28.

4   Rafaqat Hussain, 'Gwadar in Historical Perspective' Muslim Institute, https://www.muslim-institute.org.

5   Rafaqat Hussain, 'Gwadar in Historical Perspective' Muslim Institute. https://www.muslim-institute.org

6   The Baluch under the leadership of Mir Ismail defeated the Portuguese and for the following centuries they ruled over Gwadar.

7   Rafaqat Hussain, Ibid.

8   Salman Rashid, Opcit pp79-82

9   Salman Rashid Opcit p.82

10 Begum Noon was Austrian born to Christian parents, later the family moved to Britain. They enjoyed a lot of respect and political clout in their adopted country. She embraced Islam as a young lady.

11 Although Britain was not in control of South Asian subcontinent but it still enjoyed influence in Oman therefore it was deemed necessary to get British support for Pakistan.

12 According to some accounts Aga Khan paid a large sum, the remaining amount was made available by government of Pakistan.

13 Captain (Retd) Ahmed Zaheer PN 'Transfer of Gwadar to Pakistan'. The government of Pakistan assigned the task of conducting the official ceremony under the control of Vice Admiral H.M.S. Chaudhri then Commander in Chief of Pakistan Navy, Daily Time December 2020.

14 *Mehnaz Ispahani, Roads and Rivals The Politics of Access in the Borderlands of Asia*, IB Taurus London:

1989 pp 58-59.

15 Ibid.

16 Many strategists were of the view that Soviet presence in Afghanistan in 1979 was the first step which would be followed by incursion into Baluchistan which I consider to be a bit far-fetched.

17 Ibid

18 Andrew Small, *The China-Pakistan Axis Asia's New Geopolitics*, (C. Hurst Co, London 2015) p. 100.

19 Ispahani, Opcit p69.

20 Pakistan has already completed two ports on Makran coast. Ormara is a naval base and Gwadar has a dual role. Its commercial dimension is well known but along with Ormara it will provide security to CPEC's maritime trade routes. Port Qasim was second major port built by Pakistan. The advantage enjoyed by Gwadar and Ormara is that they are further away from India.

21 CPEC was formally joined by Pakistan in 2015. However, development of Gwadar began much before CPEC was launched.

22 Water sports, aquarium, restaurants specializing in sea food, museums and cultural centers along with shopping malls will be developed in the next few years.

23 Pakistan's Space and Upper Atmosphere Research Commission was established in 1961 as a Committee. It got status of Commission in 1981.

24 Brigadier (Retired) Nadir Mir, *Gwadar on the Global Chessboard*, (Ferozsons Ltd Lahore 2017) pp.38-39

25 Gwadar Smart Port City Master Plan https://www.pc.gov.pk.

26 Other areas which can be useful for Pakistan in particular can be urban planning, water resource management, gem stone and mineral resource management and food security among many other

areas of mutual interest. Dr Attaullah Shah 'China, Pakistan knowledge Corridor to prepare Pakistani youth for CPEC opportunities' Cpecinfo, 8 March 2021.

27 Mariyam Suleman, 'What Happened to Gwadar University?' *Diplomat* Brief weekly Newsletter 18 November 2020.

28 Dr Atta-ur-Rahman, 'The Knowledge Corridor', 15 June 2016 ibne_sina@hotmail.com

29 Dr Dureshewar Khan a historian I interviewed on 18 February 2022 conveyed the same message in different words. Professor Dr Attaullah Shah V.C Karakoram International University, Gilgit in his article highlighted the significance of knowledge connectivity under CPEC.

30 Dawn 1 June 2021.

31 Lucy Styles, 'Pakistan Gwadar Port' 21 January 2015, https://dlca.logeluster.org

32 Express Tribune 17 February 2021.

33 Express Tribune 17 February 2021.

34 Dawn 1 June 2021,

35 Mifrah Haq 'China builds Digital Silk Road from Pakistan to Africa and Europe, Nikkei Asia, 29 January 2021 https://asia.nikkei.com

36 Currently seven submarine cables serve Pakistan out of which four come out of India. Ibid.

37 According to one study conducted by Pakistan's Ministry of Science and Technology the coastal areas of the country have the potential to develop 50,000 Megawatts of electricity from wind. Dr Atta-ur-Rahman 'The knowledge Corridor' 15 June 2016. Email: ibne_sima@hotmail.com

38 The construction of Eastbay Expressway is necessary for the connectivity of Gwadar Port with the rest of Baluchistan. However, the residents of Khulgari have expressed reservations due to

factors enumerated above. Zofeen T. Ebrahim 'Pakistan's key CPEC Port a long way from trade hub vision' 11 August 2021 www.thethirdpole.net

39 According to some security officials the level of technological sophistication enjoyed by terrorist groups in Baluchistan has increased. They could try to neutralize the search equipment available to security forces. For this reason it is extremely essential for security forces to constantly upgrade equipment in their use. Human Intelligence operations also need to be strengthened.

40 Shahbaz Rana 'CPEC body for vacating Gwadar land.' Express Tribune, 19 February 2022.

41 Robert D. Kaplan, *Monsoon The Indian Ocean and the Future of American Power,* (Random House New York,2011) p 71.

42 Daniel Markey, *No Exit from Pakistan: America's Tortured Relationship with Islamabad.* https://www.amazon.com The concept that emerges is that the US policy is designed to keep Pakistan in a state of regulated destabilization and to keep it economically and politically dependent on the US.

43 In response to this threat Pakistan has established three more ports all West of Karachi further away from Indian territory. Port Qasim is a commercial port, Gwadar has commercial as well as naval dimension while Ormara is a naval base.

44 These scholars were from various walks of life, scientists, historians, writers and university professors no one was spared.

45 Their sponsorship of Mukti Bahin in another terrorist group has now been openly acknowledged by Indian PM Modi. RAW also promoted terrorism in Sri Lanka for many years.

46 Among Western agencies CIA and MI6 have left their footprints. Indian, some Gulf States and even

MOSSAD were mentioned.

47　Foreign adversaries have other more dangerous plans. Kaplan has suggested the secession of Baluchistan and Sindh from Pakistan for which he believes Indian support will be readily available. Such plans are more difficult to implement now due to China-Pakistan cooperation but it does reflect a dangerous mind set.

48　Kulbhushan the Indian terrorist although sentenced to death in April 2017 is still alive. India has so far executed at least three Pakistanis on similar charges.

Modern Maritime Silk Road: Geopolitical Realities in a Changing World

The term 'Modern Maritime Silk Road' (MMSR) has been introduced under the Belt and Road Initiative (BRI). This important Chinese initiative attempting to create connectivity between states for mutual benefit is designed to have two components i.e. land component popularly known as 'Modern Silk Road Economic Belt' (MSREB) and the maritime component is known as MMSR. The South China and East China Seas and Indian Ocean played pivotal role in ancient maritime Silk Road and all these maritime routes are expected to play the same role under the present setup.

Other areas which are expected to play an important role in MMSR are Mediterranean Sea and ultimately the Pacific and Atlantic Oceans. Search for cheaper and shorter maritime trade routes has led to the effort to open up Arctic Ocean.

If this venture meets with success, it could become an important link in the maritime network. Indian Ocean areas like Arabian Sea, Persian Gulf, Bay of Bengal and Strait of Malacca hold particular significance.

Throughout modern history Indian Ocean has held economic and strategic significance. It is more than 6,200 miles in length starting from southern tip of Africa and stretching to Australia. It is third largest among the five oceans of the world having an area of 27,243,000 sq miles. The deepest point is 8,047 m while the average depth is 4,741 m.

The ocean is dotted with hundreds of islands some of which hold strategic importance. Some strategic sea lanes also exist in the region, which have often been focus of rivalry among naval powers in the past. In ancient times also Chinese naval Power was reflected in economic and diplomatic spheres. Admiral Zheng He[1] made several voyages to various destinations all over the Indian Ocean reaching Sri Lanka and as far as the Arabian coast. All of his missions were peaceful projection of Chinese power, paving the way for China's trade and other peaceful activities.

The Arabs were also a great seafaring people before the advent of Islam and also after Islam spread throughout Arabia. They established small ship building ventures all over the Persian Gulf region. Also established by them were trading outposts around the Southern coast of India,

Indonesia and Malaysia. The spread of Islam to all these far off regions is often attributed to the business practices of Arab traders. They earned repute for their honesty. The Persians were also well known for their naval ventures and interest in trade and commerce.

Mughal India's share of world trade in sixteenth and seventeenth centuries was more than 27%. They had long coastlines which should have pushed them to develop a strong navy[2]; this was need of the hour, but the Mughals did not realise the importance of establishing a strong navy and ultimately paid a heavy price for their inability to do so.

Arrival of European Powers: Rivalries and the Use of Piracy

The European powers had as their focus the development of naval power even before the sixteenth century. The British, Spanish, French, Portuguese and the Dutch were in the forefront of this exercise. Spain carved out an empire in South America. The Portuguese gave tough time to them but ultimately under a settlement imposed by the church they had to shift their focus to Asia and Africa.

The British under the garb of trade with East India Company (EIC) as a front organisation, had their eyes fixed on India, Middle East and Africa. The focus of attention of France was also Middle East and Africa. The Dutch were more interested in East and Southeast Asia along with other areas producing spices. The Portuguese held some coastal areas of India and some strategic islands in the Indian Ocean.

The ostensible goal of European powers was to promote their trade and commercial activities. Since there was a power vacuum in the region, particularly lack of availability of naval power to regional states, the task of European powers became much easier.

Ottoman Turkey had a strong navy but the centre of their attention was the Mediterranean Sea and adjoining waterways. All European powers had the desire to expand their trade and to establish control over the waterways, even at the expense of other European powers. To achieve their objectives, they were ready to employ any means fair or foul.

European powers often used pirates to disrupt the trade of their rival powers. One such case was that of Britain. Under Queen Elizabeth I a system was introduced under the name of Privateers[3]. The system was based on private individuals and private vessels carrying arms[4]. The privateers were provided with documents and the task assigned to them was to disrupt the trade of rival nations. The British authorities avoided using the word 'pirate' in their case. It is a documented fact that Britain and other European nations used piracy, to undermine the commercial interests of rival powers. Francis Drake started off as a sea man who resorted to piracy off and on. Elizabeth 1 considering his special talent appointed him as a privateer. He was knighted becoming the most 'glorified' pirate of his times.

The Europeans particularly the British, fully benefitted from the lack of naval power, available to Mughals and other regional powers. The EIC came as merchants but they soon developed political ambitions. The European powers and their trading companies looked upon each other as rivals and competitors, but they also cooperated with each other whenever they had a clash with a local ruler.

The European powers acquired complete control over the Indian Ocean by the middle of sixteenth century. As already stated the European powers were not only interested in promoting their commercial interests, they were equally interested in disrupting the trade of other powers in the region.

Under Mughal emperor Jahangir the Portuguese looted a ship belonging to a prominent lady from the royal family[5]. This was not an isolated case, however, it was one that aroused the wrath of the emperor and he ordered action against the Portuguese.

During the reign of Emperor Aurangzeb, British pirates who were believed to be operating under official British patronage, looted a Mughal ship bringing pilgrims from the holy city of Macca. It was also loaded with riches, which was the main attraction for the British pirates, they also took hostages to get ransom. The British were approached but they denied that they had control over British pirates. The Commander of Mughal Naval Force in 1689 took action against Bombay Residency. The British finally agreed to pay indemnity and promised to adopt better behaviour in future[6].

The EIC ships were also attacked a few times which was probably done by pirates enjoying patronage of rival European powers. Some local element also indulged in piracy, but they did not enjoy official patronage and when caught they were duly punished.

The British after gaining dominance in the Persian Gulf adopted the goal of reducing the influence of rival European powers. They developed regional alliances with one point agenda, i.e. to cut off diplomatic ties, between Gulf States and Britain's rival states like France, Netherlands and Portugal[7].

Qawasmis the ruling family of Sharjah did not comply with British demands. The latter despite all their efforts, were unable to bend the Qawasmis, which led to their being branded as pirates. Their shipyards and commercial vessels were destroyed. It is not difficult to guess that the real purpose was to curtail capabilities, of unyielding local powers by destroying their infrastructure[8].

The British became the dominant economic power after asserting their control over regional trade. They also turned Indian Ocean into 'British Lake' by controlling all the exit and entry points in the Indian Ocean. In the east they enjoyed complete control over the of Strait of Malacca and in the west Strait of Hurmuz and Bab-el-Mandab were under their undisputed control. When the Suez Canal was established, the British were quick to assert their control over that too[9]. For the first time in the history of Indian Ocean a single power was able to control the entire ocean.

How the British accomplished this Goal

There was no significant naval power in the region and, whatever small ship building centres and other infrastructures existed, were destroyed by European powers particularly the British. The British also succeeded in eliminating various European powers gradually, ultimately establishing their full control over the Indian Ocean[10]. They also used other methods, i.e. preventing European powers from developing, diplomatic and economic relations, with Persian Gulf states. A scholarly account of these measures adopted by the Britain has been presented by Muhamad Al-Qasimi in his book *The Myth of*

Arab Piracy. The British had also developed the technological means to build big ships, they had the most modern shipyards and other facilities.

The era of European supremacy in Indian Ocean did not end suddenly, it went through a slow process of decline. But even to this day Britain, France and Portugal are in control of some strategic islands in the Indian Ocean region (IOR) British influence continued till 1967 when they finally withdrew from regions east of Suez.

After World War II US emerged as a major power in the Indian Ocean, replacing the European powers. The European powers cooperated with the US to a large extent due to the Cold War. Soviet Union the leader of the Socialist bloc, also considered Indian Ocean to be vital for maintaining their economic and political interests. However, there were many more urgent matters to deal with, like security for Soviet Union and its allies particularly in Europe. Soviet Union had few strong allies in the region, and all the deeply entrenched Western powers in the Indian Ocean, were hostile to Soviet presence in the region.

Before turning our attention to current dynamics of international politics in the region a discussion about nomenclature might be in order. The term Indian Ocean appears to be a misnomer, in the light of geographical evidence. Indian Ocean is surrounded by Africa, Asia (West Asia, South Asia, East and Southeast Asia) and Australia. Many states vital commercial, political and economic interests are linked with the IOR.

There are thirty-eight independent states surrounding the Indian Ocean, India being just one of them. Keeping historical and geographical factors in view some attempts have been made to rename the ocean. David Brewster in his book *India's Ocean: The Story of India's Bid for Regional Leadership* suggests that India is becoming an active player in the region with an assertive Policy[11]. However, there are many other actors who are also asserting their rights and interests. Mention can be made of China in this regard. Its vital commercial interests are linked to the Ocean, and for this reason, it has increased its presence in the region. An attempt on the part of any single regional state to dominate IOR, can lead to sharpening of national rivalries, further aggravating the situation.

'South Asian Ocean'[12] was suggested as a more appropriate term at a recent brain storming session in Islamabad. It appears to be comparatively more inclusive than Indian Ocean. The participants of the session were of the view that inclusiveness associated with a term should be a primary concern.

Another term which was suggested several years back is more inclusive than any other suggested so far. According to Latif Ahmed Sherwani,

'Afro-Asian Ocean' being inclusive would be far more appropriate, compared to other terms[13].

Africa's economic and geopolitical importance has increased in recent years; this phenomenon also needs to be factored into the debate about the new terminology for Indian Ocean.

Scholars are still debating as to what should be the criteria for renaming an Ocean, or any other place. Should the size of a state matter more than other considerations. An important argument revolves around the concept of inclusiveness and geographical realities. The more inclusive a term is and the degree to which it depicts geographical reality, should be important considerations according to many scholars. Though all these aspects hold academic significance, in reality changing names of places and oceans is not that easy. Even if suggested terminology appears to be superior to the existing one, it is easier to stick to status quo. Perhaps there is fear of inadvertently opening a pandora's box which holds back scholars and statesmen.

According to Braun, a narrow view of security which does not take into account aspirations and interests of littoral states, runs the risk of defeating the aims pursued by the strategists of great powers[14]. Robert P. Kaplan's view is that balance of power is changing against the West, particularly in the Indian Ocean region[15]. The rising power of China has sent shock waves all over the Western world. China's rise so far has been peaceful, even in the historical context China had largely been a peaceful state.

Due to these reasons, some scholars find it difficult, to understand Western apprehensions regarding the emergence of China as a great power. Some scholars I interviewed suggested that creating fear of China is nothing more than an effort to create unity among Western countries. According to this view point it is increasingly becoming difficult to bring US, European states and Australia on one page[16]. Some scholars believe that Western approach to China has a racial dimension. It is primarily due to this approach that West is unable to digest the emergence of China as a major power.

China's Maritime Security Strategy

It took China four decades to formulate a comprehensive maritime security strategy. This was in response to challenges posed by adversaries of China; the threatening environment created a sense of vulnerability. China's maritime strategy is in a state of evolution. It is based on an ongoing assessment of China's maritime interests and emerging challenges.

China is dependent on Indian Ocean, South China Sea and East China Sea for its international trade. Its oil and gas imports, raw materials for its industry and exports to Africa and Middle East pass through these routes. Strait of Malacca is a bottleneck which Chinese vessels have to traverse every day. For its energy security, industrial productivity and food security China is dependent on this route. The Maritime Security document [17] also highlights the linkage between China's naval strength, territorial integrity, protection of economic interests, protection of trade routes, strategic lines of communication (SLOCs) and protection of China's sovereign status.

Before 1980 China's maritime security was restricted to what is called 'Near Sea Protection'. The essence of this approach was protection of maritime security by adhering to the 'Brown Water Navy.' A low profile policy designed to maintain status quo, was preferred by the Chinese strategists in keeping with peaceful approach of China.

Reforms of 1978 brought success in every sphere of national life and made more resources available to the strategists. In 1993 the Yinke incident appeared to undermine the maritime security of China.[18] The country could not be left at the mercy of arrogant hostile powers. The new approach led to the decision in 2012 to build a strong maritime force. Since then there has been qualitative and quantitative improvement in capabilities of PLA (N).

There are some major changes which have taken place in China's naval strategy. Mention was made earlier regarding Admiral Zheng He's visits to ports in SCS and Indian Ocean which clearly shows that historically China had interest in both these areas. The difference is that now China has adopted a clear 'two oceans policy.' The Pacific Ocean and the Indian Ocean will now be the main focus of China. Port facilities will be developed in both regions with the objective of strengthening Chinese presence and capabilities. The adoption of two ocean policy will enable Chinese navy to protect its trade routes in a much better way. Development of ports in the region is an essential requirement for this purpose and several steps have been taken in this regard.

China has now opted for a 'Blue Water Navy' which was required for a more effective protection of China's maritime interests in far off regions. The Yinke incident clearly highlighted the linkage between a strong navy and, security of economic and trade interests in far off regions of the world. In terms of number of naval ships, their technological sophistication, and policy of national self-reliance China has made great strides. 'Far Sea Protection' has replaced the earlier policy of 'Near Sea Protection. All these changes reflect a widening of vision, which covers every aspect of Chinese policy.

There are several schools of thought in the PLA (N). Two of these are more significant. The Mahanian school is believed to favour the creation of blue water navy, which has come into being since

1980. It is better equipped to protect China's long term and short-term maritime interests in far off waters. It is also believed by Western experts that the Mahanian school prefers establishment of off shore naval bases. However, in reality China has so far established only one naval base in Digi bouti[19]. The other ports developed by China are only for commercial purposes. Land reclamation activities are also favoured by the Mahanian school according to Edward Chan. Chan further states that the Chinese naval strategists belonging to this school favour the establishment of Chinese control over the sea lanes[20].

However, there is little evidence to suggest that Chinese navy is interested in controlling the sea lanes, or to exclude other powers from peaceful use of these sea lanes. It seems reasonable to assume, that China will assert its ability to have free access to sea lanes, without excluding other nations from using these for peaceful purposes. Unless forced by circumstances China will not opt for military bases in the future also.

The other major school is Harmonious school, which believes that China must cooperate with other navies, in the task of global maritime governance. Law enforcement in blue waters, is also an important aspect, of what the Chinese navy is doing to shoulder its international responsibilities[21]. It regularly participates in AMAN naval exercise arranged by Pakistan navy on biennial basis. One of the goals of this endeavor is to coordinate action against piracy. Diplomatic activities, engaging in negotiations if necessary and, activities like participating in naval exercises and calling on ports of friendly states, are subsumed in this frame-work. Giving protection to Chinese fishermen and other activities in support of civilians, for example evacuation of civilians in times of crises, are also considered important. Resource exploitation in international waters is also given special significance by the Chinese navy.

The number of maritime actors and activities has increased in recent years. PLA (N) has assumed full responsibility for defending territorial integrity and, China's economic interests in far away waters as well. Coast Guards are actively engaged in pursuing their responsibilities defending the coast and ensuring security. As already pointed out there is a wide variety of activities undertaken by major actors in maritime sector. These include Grey Zone operations like diplomacy, International Peace Operations including anti-drug and anti-piracy operations. Also included in the category are other humanitarian operations. Above all normal defense in the maritime sector, keeping in view defensive and if need be offensive operations to defeat enemy designs are included.

Power projection is also included among the responsibilities of PLA (N). Initially the approach was 'Responsive' but since Yinke incident the

Chinese navy has opted for a more 'Proactive' and assertive role.

China is helping developing states to build and further develop their sea ports, mostly for commercial purposes. Myanmar's Kyaupyu port has benefitted from Chinese assistance. China is also developing Coco Islands belonging to Myanmar. India is fearful that China would use Coco Islands to keep an eye on India's military bases in the region. India is itself engaging in efforts to spy on China. Chinese facilities in Coco Islands and Kyaupyu will make China less vulnerable to US-India nexus in the region.

China also plans to link Andaman Sea with South China Sea, by digging a canal in Kra Isthmus which is part of Thailand[22]. A number of overhead bridges and road networks are also planned. China will certainly benefit but so will developing states in South and Southeast Asian region.

Bangladesh (BD) does not share land border with China, therefore when it decided to join BRI India did not allow access to it. However, China and BD have found a way to circumvent the Indian hurdle. Chittagong port of BD is being developed by China, as a result of which China will get access to another port in the Indian Ocean[23]. Sri Lanka's Hambantota port developed by China has been leased to it for 99 years[24]. This will further enhance Chinese presence in the Indian Ocean.

Another port to have been developed by China is a natural deep-sea port at Gwadar (Baluchistan province of Pakistan) It has already become operational and is being run by a Chinese Company. This port is expected by experts to become an economic hub in near future. The factories in Xinjian (Western China) will have a much shorter route to their markets through the port of Gwadar. China's import of oil, gas and other raw materials will also be transported to China through Gwadar. Gwadar is a modern port with all the facilities like ware houses, road networks and special economic zones[25].

The network of ports developed by China are often referred to as 'String of Pearls' by Western media. The term was coined by a consulting firm Booz Allen Hamilton in 2004. These ventures are commercial in nature but the Washington Post incorrectly labeled it as Chinese Security paradigm[26]. Whether they will remain purely commercial ventures, or develop a military dimension, will depend on a number of factors. If rival powers choose to challenge China with their military might, then China in order to protect its interests, might opt for a military response. China does not prefer military alliances; but in view of emerging military challenges, China might change its approach. Establishment of military bases and alliances might be adopted as a policy under an extreme scenario.

China and the South China Sea:

South China Sea is important for all the regional states particularly China as 80% of its trade currently passes through SCS[27]. It makes China vulnerable to action from rival powers also in the Strait of Malacca. China's policy in SCS is based on nine-dash policy.

In 1948 just before the end of civil war leading to the victory of Communist forces the 'Nationalist government' issued a map based on 'eleven dashes. It declared sovereignty and the right to maritime resources over the islands and reefs within the lines[28]. After the establishment of Peoples Republic of China over the whole of Chinese main land, the new government endorsed the idea of eleven-dash lines and sovereignty over land, water and resources contained in the U-shaped dashed line.

According to Liu Zhen, China's ownership of land and other resources, is based on historical maritime rights. He has also claimed that the U-shaped dash line constitutes 90% of the contested waters[29].

The original eleven segments were modified in 1952 to nine when Mao Tse Tung allowed Vietnam to take over two segments in the Gulf of Tonkin as a friendly gesture[30]. Article 2 para 2 of Law on Territorial Sea and the Contiguous Zone of 25 February 1992 states that PRC's territorial land includes the mainland and its offshore islands,

Taiwan and the various affiliated islands including Diaoyu Island, Penghu Island, Dongsha Island, Xisha Island, Nansha (Spratly) Island and other islands belonging to PRC. Article 14 of the EEZ and Continental Shelve Act refers to historical rights[31].

An 81-year-old Chinese scholar is reported to have said that all the lines have a scientific basis. The line is broken up because it is a maritime boundary. It is not a fixed borderline on land. The lines reflect humanitarian spirit as China allows neighbouring states to pass through it without hindrance[32].

There are several disputes in the SCS between regional states. The US policy of exploiting these disputes to its own advantage has aggravated tension in the region. US Secretary of State Hillary Clinton visited Hanoi in 2010. She proclaimed a few principles, some of these appeared to be controversial, while others seemed ambiguous and did not help in the process of conflict resolution. According to my analysis they had the effect of sharpening rhetoric. This has created the impression that the US does not wish to see China gain control over the areas which have historically been part of its territory. But instead of getting directly involved in a conflict with China the US wants to use regional states for that purpose[33].

US views China's policy of creating artificial island in SCS as highly unacceptable and accuses China of militarising them China like other countries attaches great importance to defending territories that belong to it. These islands are seen as first line of defense by the Chinese. The Chinese Naval Chief Wu Shengli in his meeting with US Chief of Naval Operations informed him that China will continue its policy of converting sea reefs into artificial islands with basic military facilities[34].

China's Arctic Silk Road

China under the 14th five-year plan covering 2020-2025, has launched the idea of developing sea routes for trade and commerce, in the Arctic region. Due to global warming ice has started melting which has made it possible to develop marine trade routes in the Arctic Ocean. China, Russia and other states in the Arctic region will be cooperating with each other under the Chinese initiative. The idea behind the move is to transform China's land and sea connections to Europe and beyond. China plans to build infrastructure of ports, roads and railway lines connecting various parts of Eurasian regions.

There are several possibilities which have aroused the interest of China. The Transpolar Sea Route (TSR) can connect the Atlantic Ocean with the Pacific. If this idea gains ground it will cut across the centre of Arctic Ocean passing close to the North Pole. It can lead to reduction in distances but it remains frozen most of the year and is therefore harder to cross.

The two Arctic shipping routes currently available i.e the North Sea Route and the Northwest passage are currently the most feasible alternatives according to South China Morning Post of Hong Kong. China is so far the only country to have launched official expeditions in all three Arctic shipping passages[35].

China plans in the next few years to expand its activities in the Arctic region. White Paper published in 2018 presents a detailed blue print of how things will proceed. All the schemes will be integrated to launch a bigger project under the title of Polar Silk Road. This will be part of BRI to facilitate trade and other activities of BRI member states[36].

It is evident now that in the next eight or ten years, the Arctic Ocean may be free of ice during summer months. Potentially there are three routes which can be created in the Arctic. The Northeast Passage around Eurasia can reduce the shipping time between China and Netherlands by three weeks[37]. This route suits the interests of China as it can promote trade and reduce expenses.

The Northwest Passage goes around North America and the third route passes through central Arctic Ocean. All these routes suit China as they offer shorter and cheaper alternatives to current shipping routes. China's interest in the Arctic region involves more than just a quest for new trade routes. Oil, gas and mineral deposits are known to exist, particularly oil and gas along the Russian coast. Another factor which suits Russia is that ice is melting fastest along Northeast Passage which touches Russian coast line.

The idea of working with Russia to turn Northeast Passage into Arctic Silk Road was first proposed by China in July 2017. The backbone of this economic cooperation is shipping, energy and scientific research[38]. The development plans which have been unveiled so far mostly concern energy development, port construction and infrastructure development.

China, Russia and France decided to work together on Yamal LNG project. Production started in December 2017. It is world's largest LNG project and first joint Arctic Silk Road venture launched by China and Russia.

Payakha Oilfield development venture was initiated by China and Russia in June 2019. China National Chemical Engineering Group and Russian firm Neftegaz Holding signed a deal planning an investment of 5bn US dollars over a period of four years. A second Arctic Silk Road energy project is also under consideration, under this six crude oil processing facilities, a port to handle 50 million tons of oil a year, oil pipelines, power station and oil storage facilities are envisaged[39].

Zarubino port will be developed under a deal signed between China and Russia. Its major attraction is that it will be ice free round the year. It is located Southwest of Vladivostok close to Chinese border. After completion it will be largest port in Northeast Asia. Its capacity will be 60 million tons of cargo a year. Railway line will be laid to link it up with Northeast China, strengthening NE China's link with the rest of the world. Russia's far eastern region will also benefit[40].

Arkhangelsk a deep-sea port project is in planning stage. It is the largest city on Russia's Northern coast on European side close to Finland. Another port which is also in planning stage is 55 Km from Arkhangelsk. It will be linked up with Russian railway net-work. It will consolidate Russia's link with Siberia. It is also expected to create 40,000 jobs.

China Institute of Remote Sensing and Digital Earth signed an agreement with Finland's Arctic Space Centre. The purpose of this venture is climate research, environmental monitoring and Arctic navigation. The Centre will contribute to China's 'Digital Silk Road' plan. It will create spatial information system for BRI.

China-Iceland Arctic Science Observatory was established in October 2018. It is managed by Polar Research Institute of China and Institute of Research Centres of Iceland. The fields of cooperation are atmosphere, oceans, glaciers, geophysics, remote sensing and biology[41].

China's Modern Maritime Silk Road concept is designed to promote trade and other peaceful activities for mutual benefit. Keeping the emerging challenges in perspective, China has built its naval strength in a pragmatic manner.

US Role in Indian Ocean and South China Sea: Role of Allies

The US, other Western states and Asian allies of US take the rise of China as a formidable challenge. The Chinese economy is already second largest and there are forecasts that within the next few years it will leave the US behind. China used its resources judiciously to expand and modernise its defense forces. The US is particularly concerned about the increasing capabilities of PLA (N). China's influence and soft power were greatly enhanced as a result of launching of BRI, which currently includes more than forty states. According to the original plan sixty-five to eighty states will ultimately be part of the scheme.

The US has followed a two-pronged approach; BRI is the target of intense propaganda in order to dissuade states from joining it. If this approach does not work, then regime change has been tried by US, without realizing that it is illegal and unlawful for a state to promote regime change in another state. The US has also recently launched infrastructure projects of its own, something it had ignored before BRI was launched by China. Most have been discussed in Chapter dealing with Silk Road Economic Belt.

The schemes launched by US have two major dimensions, the economic component has attracted some states. On the other hand, the plans to bring states together for cooperation in military ventures, has not been that popular. There are several factors which prevent regional states from joining the US sponsored military alliances. These factors will be explored as we proceed ahead.

Traditionally the US followed two ocean policy. Atlantic Ocean was important in the context of relations with European powers. US trade with European states and the issue of security did not allow any deviation. The US started expanding westward, annexing more and more territory. As a result of this expansion the US got access to the Pacific Ocean. US occupied several islands in the Pacific Ocean, as they had done in the Atlantic Ocean several decades back. Needless to say that many of these islands gave strategic edge to the US against its rival nations. Asian states lying on the other side of Pacific Ocean were considered to be important in military as well as economic sense. It was US goal to acquire military ascendency in the Pacific region, while at the same time asserting control over the Indian Ocean.

In the post-World War II scenario with the outbreak of Cold War, US found a favorable environment to further extend its influence. Soviet Union's influence had to be reduced at every cost. George Kenan was the author of the policy of containment which was applied against Soviet Union. Most of the European powers decided to reduce their presence in the Indian Ocean, which convinced the US to expand their role in the region. During Cold War US was able to establish naval bases in the Persian Gulf, Western Indian Ocean and Southeast Asia including Philippines and Thailand. They also established military bases on land under treaties likes SEATO and CENTO. The Middle East attracted the US due to the abundance of oil and gas in the region. The US wanted to acquire the ability to deny these resources to its adversaries. Soviet Union also maintained strong political relation with several Arab states[42].

In late 1960s UK decided to withdraw from areas east of Suez. Before leaving Mauritius they separated the island of Diego Garcia from it. The US wanted to establish a multi-purpose military base in the region. They were looking for a suitable site but they informed UK that the island should be cleared of people. The people were driven out of their homes without even compensation for the loss of their homes. This is one of the greatest violations of human rights committed by Western powers in recent times. Since late 1960s the US has established a full-fledged military base in Diego Garcia. It was used by US in its aggression against Afghanistan and Iraq[43].

As is well known China introduced a series of economic and political reforms in 1978. The economy was opened up, foreign multinationals came up with substantial investments and Chinese multinationals emerged in subsequent years. Poverty was eradicated and the success of China in the economic sphere, provided a ray of hope for other developing countries. The Chinese model of development has kindled hopes that if developing states followed the model, they too could succeed in breaking the cycle of poverty and underdevelopment.

The optimism aroused by the rise of China in the third world countries is not appreciated by many Western states. The US and its close allies look upon the emergence of China as a source of threat. Several initiatives have been launched by the US to counter BRI and contain China. There is preponderance of initiatives which carry a military dimension, but it would be simplistic to say that other dimensions are totally missing. Some initiatives do carry economic or political dimensions.

Obama's presidency is remembered for some of the approaches launched by him and his Secretary of State Hillary Clinton. In order to contain China it was considered necessary to shift the focus of US policy to Asia[44]. The 'Pivot to Asia' and 'Asia Rebalance' were launched by the Obama administration. Both these initiatives have one objective and that is to contain China's rise as a great power. Under 'Pivot to Asia' and 'Rebalance to Asia' the idea is to turn the focus of attention to Asia. While Soviet Union existed and Cold War was on, Europe could not be ignored and Middle East also held importance because of oil and gas.

The fear of growing Soviet influence in the oil rich region was a source of discomfort for the US. Having won the Cold War after disintegration of Soviet Union, the US is now trying to focus its attention on containment of China. Asia is to become the primary focus and India is seen as part of the larger strategy to contain China. Another essential element in the containment strategy is to create linkage between Indian Ocean and Pacific Ocean.

The idea of linking 'Indo-pacific' region was suggested by Japanese Prime-Minister Shinzo Abe in 2007. As stated earlier the idea is to integrate Indian Ocean with Pacific Ocean in order to promote US hegemony over the whole region[45]. It is a vast region and according to an article appearing in Foreign Affairs the author Van Jackson maintains that under Joe Biden a new position has been added to the National Security Council. The newly created position known as 'Indo-Pacific Coordinator' was filled by Kurt Cambell. The Pacific Command has now been renamed as 'Indo-Pacific Command'. The historic focus of Pentagon has moved away from Europe and West Asia to South, Southeast and East Asia extending all the way to US. According to the author Indian Ocean's significance was realized by the US strategists particularly after the publication of a ground breaking book on Indian Ocean by Robert D. Kaplan in 2010[46].

According to Jackson the concept of 'Indo-Pacific' carries a number of problems. The US has built its dominant position in the Pacific region over a period covering at least two centuries, while its role in Indian Ocean is relatively new having started after World War II. Shifting Focus away from Atlantic and Pacific (where US is strong) to Indian Ocean without clear gains in sight would not be prudent[47]. This could also result in overstretch which could be detrimental to the interests of US, but perhaps beneficial for US allies. At present there are few people in Pentagon and the US State Department to take Jackson's criticism seriously.

Indo-pacific region includes the entire region from the western coast of India to the eastern coast of US. The idea is to include India in the Indo-Pacific region. In order to contain and counterbalance China, one of the steps taken by the US is launching of Quadrilateral Security Dialogue commonly known as Quad. The US, Japan, Australia and India are members of Quad. The Quad has been designed to improve naval cooperation and coordination between member states in order to contain China[48].

A number of naval exercises were organised by Quad in order to promote coordination between naval forces of member states. Achieving interoperability is another major objective of these exercises. The one which took place in April 2021 was joined by France. According to media reports some European countries including Germany, UK and France are expected to join Quad. Efforts are underway to convince some ASEAN countries including Malaysia, Vietnam and Philippines to join the Quad thus converting it into Quad Plus. The Chinese have sad memories of US, Russia, Japan, Australia and various European powers having invaded China at various times in history particularly in 1900[49]. For many Chinese strategists Quad evokes memories of the aggressions which took place in the past.

Malabar Naval exercises are organised by India on regular basis. A number of countries which are politically close to the US coordinated with India in this venture. Although Malabar Naval exercise is separate from Quad but all members of this alliance join the naval exercise. The difference is therefore purely academic. The Quad is seen as Asian NATO of the future. This clearly suggests that Quad is a military venture no matter how hard India and the West try to dispel this impression. The goal of creating a new 'military balance of power favorable to the US' is the real objective of Quad[50].

The difference between 'Asia-Pacific' and 'Indo-Pacific' is at the root of emerging rivalries in the Asian region. 'Asia-Pacific' refers to the Asian states facing the Pacific Ocean while 'Indo-Pacific' refers to the US desire to link up the Indian Ocean with the Pacific Ocean, in order to pool the resources of states in both regions, to contain China. This also aims at convincing states in 'Indo-Pacific' to share the financial burden with the US.

The US an extra regional power has tried to create problems for China in SCS and ECS. Regional disputes are being exploited and the Western fear of a rising Asian power, is also being used to generate support for US policies. The US accuses China of creating artificial islands in the region in order to use them for military purposes. US, Australia, Japan and India along with some European powers are trying to exert military pressure on China in its own backyard[51].

Viewed from China's perspective SCS and ECS are essential for its economic survival and, the steps taken by it are purely defensive. It also regards the presence of extra regional powers and their pressure tactics against China as manifestation of aggressive intent.

Dr Claude an Australian scholar believes that there could be a military show down in the region. It could occur sooner than expected either on the issue of Taiwan or the Sea Lanes in the region. This development if it occurs, could have long term consequences for the region and the world. If the US is perceived after the show down, as a power which was unable to achieve its major military objectives, its status as a super power will suffer a setback. Therefore, in his view US will go all out in a conflict of this nature[52].

On the other hand, Admiral (Retired) Pervaiz Asghar (PN) refuted the possibility of an armed clash between the two powers. According to him both powers have so far avoided direct military confrontation and they will continue to do so in future also[53]. Another factor to bear in mind is that in relative terms, US naval capabilities have declined in comparison to China, over the last few years. Over the last couple of decades PLA (N) has emerged as a modern fighting force. It has expanded while at the same time there has been technological upgradation of weapon systems. The gap between the two navies has narrowed down and in near future Chinese navy is expected to surpass the US Navy[54].

Quad's ability to play an important role in regional politics would depend on a number of factors. US reputation has been a cause for concern particularly after their defeat in Afghanistan. The chaotic exit from Kabul is still fresh in public mind in the US and abroad.

According to Italian scholar Dr. Troiani while Trump was in power, many European states and other allies of US, were concerned about lack of consistency in US approach. However, when Biden was elected perceptions of many European leaders began to change[55]. It seems that the chaotic scenes of Trump's departure from Washington D.C have already been forgotten by some European leaders. They expect Mr Biden to regain the confidence of European allies.

The frequency of US involvement in overseas wars, which it invariably failed to win and at times outrightly lost, has to a large extent eroded international confidence in US ability to lead. The propensity to launch wars and to exaggerate perceptions of military threat, serves the interests of arms manufacturers, it also results in overstretch which can erode US status as a super power.[56]

Australia signed a deal with France to acquire French built submarines. The French called it deal of the century but in 2021, Australia unilaterally scrapped the deal with France and signed a security pact with UK and US. AUKUS is a security pact between the three English speaking nations. Under this deal Australia will acquire eight nuclear powered submarines from its partners. France has lost the opportunity to earn billions of dollars which will now go to US and UK. France considers this to be a stab in the back[57].

There are two dimensions of the new deal which have been criticised. Will the new deal breach nuclear non-proliferation regulations? According to one view the deal is dangerous as it provides nuclear technology to Australia which is otherwise a non-nuclear nation. This view is shared by several states. The Australian view point is that there is no breach of prevailing regulations, as the submarines are nuclear powered, but do not have the capacity to carry nuclear weapons. Nuclear powered submarines are much faster and can remain under water much longer, compared to a non-nuclear-powered submarine. It is therefore quite obvious that Australia's naval power will be greatly strengthened and this could lead to a naval arms race in the region.

The creation of AUKUS has revealed a faultline in the Western alliance. The Western powers stand together on many global issues. On the issue of economic inequality, under development, poverty and unfair terms of trade faced by developing countries the Western states stand united against Asian and African states. The rise of China is also perceived as a challenge by them, but when it comes to pursuing their own national interests, the cracks in the alliance become visible and the English-speaking nations stand out as a bloc[58]. However, there are some exceptions too, New Zealand has announced that it will not allow nuclear submarines from Australia and other nations to call on New Zealand ports[59].

Five English speaking Western nations have organized an intelligence net-work covering Indian Ocean and other regions. This is an artifact of their net-work which was organised during World War II and continued to play an important role during the era of Cold War. Five Eyes includes intelligence agencies of Canada, US, UK, Australia and New Zealand (FVEY) Five Eyes remains as a core group around which other nations have been allowed to make their contribution. Nine Eyes include the Five Eyes along with Denmark, France, Netherlands and Norway. Now Germany, Belgium, Italy, Sweden and Spain have also joined leading to formation of Fourteen Eyes[60].

The idea behind forming a multinational intelligence gathering network is attractive as it helps these states to pool their financial and other resources. Intelligence gathered is shared. Since there are many states involved in the task of gathering intelligence none stands out and all benefit. For intelligence operations to be effective understanding of cultural environment is necessary. In the past (and perhaps even now) foreign missionaries played a significant role in this field. Kaplan has mentioned individuals with expertise in culture and politics of Myanmar who would be ready to work for US and other Western intelligence agencies[61].

They have not been mentioned by name of course. This is a potential source of threat for Myanmar and other developing states. If they are destabilised it could have negative impact on BRI. Kaplan has also tried to focus US attention on 'Chinese intelligence operations' in Myanmar, which in my opinion are designed to protect their interests and those of Myanmar, against the activities of rival intelligence agencies. It is in China's interest to have stable states in the region.

Regional States Maritime Strategies

Pakistan's naval strategy is the result of challenges posed by India. Indian designs play a major part in determining Pakistan's security environment. The challenge and response are intertwined. Pakistan's coast line is relatively short and when it gained independence there was only one port in the Western wing. Karachi was a commercial as well as a naval port even before independence. On two occasions India tried to blocade Karachi port. During the 1971 Pakistan-India war and also during the Kargil crisis, the Indian navy tried to put economic and military pressure on Pakistan, by blocking the only port available to the country at that time. Pakistan learnt two lessons from this Indian move. Pakistan needed more commercial ports and naval bases to secure its coast line, territorial waters and economic interests. Another important conclusion was that allies should be encouraged to have outlet into the Indian Ocean.

Port Qasim[62] was built by Fauji Foundation of Pakistan. It is spread over 350 acres and has been built at a cost of 370 million dollars. In June 1973 the parliament passed an Act under which Port Qasim was built. It is 58.1 Km west of Karachi. The port started operations in 1980 becoming the main centre for importing material for Pakistan Steel Mills.

Another major project was launched to provide security to Pakistan's commercial and other interests. Jinnah Naval Base has been established and became operational in 1988. The base at Ormara is fully operational second naval base of Pakistan. Since the inception of CPEC the major function of the naval base is to provide security to Pakistani, Chinese and other commercial vessels in the region.

Gwadar port has emerged as a major natural deep sea port. One of its roles is to facilitate the trade of China with West Asia and Africa. Afghanistan and Central Asian states are also eager to use Gwadar to facilitate their trade. Gwadar is Pakistan's third commercial port; it also houses a naval base for strengthening Pakistan's maritime security. Although China and Pakistan have so far not signed a defense treaty but PLA(N) ships will be allowed to dock when the two countries so desire.

Pakistan navy is modernising its ship building and submarine manufacturing facilities, with the help of China and Turkiye. As already stated giving protection to Chinese and Pakistani commercial vessels will be the responsibility of Pakistan navy. Coastal highways and other road networks, connecting north with south and east with west are also being developed.

Naval diplomacy has taken many different forms but AMAN series are the most prominent venture in this regard. It is biennial naval exercise which has received favourable press coverage in Pakistan and abroad. The most recent was in February

2023 in which more than fifty navies participated including China, Russia, Turkiye, Iran, Saudi Arabia, Japan, Australia and US[63]. Some of these navies have not worked together for decades but they came together under the banner of AMAN. Warships, aircraft, Special Operation Forces and a large number of observers participated in the naval exercises.

India was absent as it was not invited. The purpose of naval exercise, whether AMAN or any other, is to promote coordination of naval strategies of the participating navies. Other major goals are to improve fighting capability of naval forces and to promote cooperation against piracy. Pakistan will not submit to Indian naval domination and would not permit India, to use its naval power to blockade Pakistani ports. Cooperation between Pakistani navy and PLA (N) is in mutual interest and is expected to grow further in future.

Indian Naval Strategy

India is following the advice of a well-known Indian naval strategist K.M. Panikkar who suggested that Indian Ocean should be fully under India's control[64]. According to him Indian Ocean should be converted into an 'Indian Lake' which should be the main goal of India[65]. Panikkar also suggested that it should be the policy of India to exclude all extra regional powers from the Indian Ocean. Only then will India be able to establish its uncontested control over the ocean. When the US established a naval base at Diego Garcia India opposed the move on two grounds. Firstly, it believed that so long as extra regional forces are active in the region Indian dream of dominating IOR will be difficult to achieve. Secondly, at that time India was a close ally of the Soviet Union and therefore, it viewed the development in the context of Cold War.

Now in view of emerging China-US rivalry India has decided to join the US in containing China. India is now a strategic ally of US and, the two have been holding strategic dialogue on yearly basis. The purpose is to coordinate their security policies, the main plank of which is containment of China. The two countries have also been holding joint naval exercises. Indian controlled group of islands at the mouth of Strait of Malacca have been militarized and US has been given access to them. Port Blair in South Andaman serves as the capital of Andaman and Nicobar groups of islands called Indian Union territories. Personnel from India's armed forces form part of Andaman and Nicobar Command, India's first and only tri-service command which was set up in 2001.

The main purpose behind this according to Lintner was to keep a keen eye on China's maritime activities in the region. Sanat Kaur has drawn a similar conclusion[66]. India claims to be concerned about Myanmar's Coco Islands, which it believes are being developed by China to not only facilitate its trade and political activities, but to have a military edge over its adversaries.

India's over ambitious policies in IOR are bound to cause serious concern to other regional states like Pakistan and China. This could lead to increased tensions in the region.

Role of Islands in the Indian Ocean, SCS and ECS

Islands have often played an important role in history by determining the naval strategies of nations. The Indian Ocean is dotted with thousands of islands. There are island states like Madagascar which is the largest island in the region. Sri Lanka, Maldives and Mauritius are some other strategic islands. Diego Garcia as stated earlier was part of Mauritius before UK the occupying power, detached it from Mauritius and handed it over to the US, to build a military base. Seychelles also holds geostrategic importance in the context of new Cold War being launched by US to contain China. Indonesia is composed of hundreds of islands big and small. Malaysia, Myanmar, Australia and India also exercise control over some strategic islands[67].

There are a number of island disputes in the Persian Gulf. Ever since 1971 Iran and UAE have experienced serious dispute over Abu Musa and Larger and Lesser Tunb. Iraq and Iran also have a dispute since 1973 regarding Bubiyan and warba two important islands which neither party would let go.

In SCS and ECS one would notice large number of islands. Taiwan is an island which China regards to be its integral part and history supports that argument. China also owns several dozen islands in the region some of which are natural and others are artificial. Japan falls in a category of its own. It is an important island state not only in the region but globally it is accorded great importance.

The Western colonial powers operating in the Indian Ocean region, realized the strategic importance of some of these islands and, were quick to assert their control over them. It would not be wrong to say that naval rivalries between European powers often focused around these Islands. Most islands won their freedom but others were not so lucky. Some islands in IOR still find themselves under Western occupation mention may be made of Diego Garcia. The military base has been used by the US in its wars of aggression against Iraq and Afghanistan.

Mention can also be made of British Indian Ocean territories (BIOT). France also has islands under its control. La Reunion, Mayotte and Antarctic territories are considered to be part of France. As the case of Diego Garcia clearly indicates, the Western nations often handed over the control of islands to each other, even against the wishes of local people, leading to eviction from their homes and territory.

States enjoying sovereignty over islands acquire many advantages eg extension in limit of territorial waters and exclusive economic zone. These states get additional maritime resources and the strategic benefits are in addition to all this. India's control over Andaman and Nicobar islands has given it tremendous advantage including the ability to block the Strait of Malacca. However, under the changing geostrategic scenario, this may not be a major bargaining chip, as China is less dependent on Malacca compared to a few years back. China has developed several options so as not to be restricted to any one approach.

It should be remembered though that, US has access to Indian military bases in Andaman and Nicobar, which could have the effect of strengthening its position in Eastern Indian Ocean. To balance that China has signed an agreement with Myanmar, to gain access to strategically placed Coco Island, which would balance off US-India advantage in Andaman Sea.

India has belatedly realized the importance of island nations and has already launched its own version of 'Island diplomacy'[68]. Indian Prime Minister Modi visited some island nations in IOR. His official tour took him to Sri Lanka, Maldives, Mauritius, Seychelles and Madagascar. The 2015 tour of Modi was rare in the sense, that after many decades an Indian PM undertook a visit, in the context of India's growing discomfort over the rise of China as a major player in the Indian Ocean. India has offered weapons and military support to some of these nations. It is also looking for an opportunity to establish military base in Seychelles, and if possible, in some other strategic islands too. China too has cordial relations with the island nations mentioned above. If they join BRI in the next year or so, it will be mutually beneficial for all the parties. There are two factors which do not go in India's favour. There is a trust deficit between India and its smaller neighbours. Mutual trust is absolutely essential for political relations to flourish. Another major factor which cannot be discounted, is that India does not have the financial and other resources, required to meet the challenge. China's resources cannot be matched by India. Even US is unable to help India in this regard. China can help regional states to modernize their infrastructure which would promote regional trade and poverty alleviation.

Socotra an island belonging to Yemen also enjoys strategic location. The island has been recently occupied by UAE. At several webinars and video conferences held during the last two years, scholars expressed fear that in-view of UAE's close relations with Israel and India, if it hands over the island to either country, it will carry adverse consequences for Pakistan and China. In either case it would be detrimental to Pakistan's long term interests making Gwadar vulnerable.

However, Ambassador (Retired) Syed Hasan Javed had a rather different perspective on the subject. He rightly believes that it is no more possible for a state to permanently occupy the territory belonging to another state. When hostilities in Yemen come to an end UAE will be bound by International Law to return possession of the islands back to Yemen.

China-Solomon Island Pact

China has recently signed a pact with Solomon Islands in Southern Pacific Ocean. A hype has been created in the US led alliance regarding this development. The US, Australia, India and Japan along with some European allies have been critical of this move. The impression the US has been trying to create is that China is developing a naval base under the new agreement. The Chinese side has denied this accusation. They have stated on more than one occasion that they are not interested in establishing military bases in the region. The Solomon Islands government has also denied that the agreement carries military clauses. Under the arrangement China will get access to facilities for refueling of vessels, occasional port calls and other commercial facilities like access to warehouses etc[69].

The US government now claims that it has had historical links with Southern Pacific Ocean region, but current history disproves their claims. They basically ignored the region for several decades expecting Australia to play the leading role. Since 1993 US has not even maintained diplomatic relations with Solomon Islands[70].

The government of Solomon Islands expects the deal to be mutually beneficial. In the past there has been a lot of foreign interference and, attempts at regime change in Solomon Islands. Not having a proper police force to maintain domestic peace was a cause of weakness. The government was dependent on Australian riot police to help it in establishing internal peace. China has offered to help Solomon Island in establishing a proper police force. The training and equipment will be provided by China. China's soft power will increase further and Chinese influence in the region will be consolidated. China expects Solomon Islands and other regional states to play an important role in BRI.

Modern Maritime Silk Road is an important aspect of Belt and Road Initiative launched by China. It would not be an exaggeration to state that the success of BRI depends to a large extent, on how the maritime dimension evolves in the next few years. The adversaries of China mainly US, UK, India and Australia also regard MMSR to be a crucial factor in determining the success of BRI. It is for this reason that they are devising policies to target various dimensions of the maritime belt.

Their efforts have so far not met with success due to a combination of factors. The planning part of

US and its allies appears to carry some inherent weaknesses. To give just one example, different US administrations launched initiatives, which were often abandoned by the next administration. The new administration was far more interested in launching its own programme, than in completing the project launched by the earlier administration. Lack of consistency and inadequate allocation of resources are also responsible for the apparent lack of success of US initiatives.

Compared to this the Chinese initiatives are based on meticulous planning and, have greater appeal for developing states that dream of a better future for their people.

Chapter VII

1   Admiral Zheng He served the Ming dynasty. The route he followed was part of ancient maritime Silk Road. He followed the Islamic faith.

2   Mughals took pride in constructing beautiful palaces, other buildings and gardens. They also established educational institutions although that was not the top priority.

3   Deepthi Murali Episode 13 European Pirates in the Indian Ocean, 2 October 2020 https://www.masalahistory.com She has mentioned names of several British pirates who were given the task to attack and loot Spanish ships. They did not spare Mughal and other Indian ships either.

4   Nick kolakowski 'The King of Pirates and the Biggest Pirate Heist in History', 16 February 2018 https://weolakowski.modium.com also see golden age of piracy https://en.m.wikipedia.org

5   The Portuguese introduced the 'Pass System'. It was a method of collecting tax without authority. Any ship without 'Pass' was fair game for the Portuguese.

6   Ellison B. Findlay 'The Capture of Maryam-uz-Zamani's Ship: Mughal Women and European traders', *Journal of the American Oriental Society* Vol 108, no2 (April-June 1988)

7   Mohammad Al-Qasimi, *The Myth of Arab Piracy*, (Routledge N.Y 1986). p31.

8   Ibid.

9   The idea was first conceived by the French but by virtue of their control over Egypt the British gained control over Suez Canal.

10 Qasimi in his scholarly work has presented several examples of British interference in Persian Gulf states relations with various European powers.

11 David Brewster, '*India's Ocean: The Story of India's Bid for Regional Leadership*', (Routledge, N.Y 2010).

12 Recently at a conference in Islamabad the term 'South Asian Ocean' has also been suggested.

13 Latif Ahmed Sherwani at a seminar in Georgetown University Washington DC suggested the term 'Afro-Asian Ocean in March 1971. Similarly Rashida Poonawala writing for Pakistan Horizon in 1974 suggested the same term.

14 Dieter Braun, 'The Indian Ocean in Afro-Asian Perspective', JSTOR (The World Today), vol 28, No 6 (June 1972) p. 249

15 Robert D. Kaplan, *Monsoon the Indian Ocean and the Future of American Power*, (Random House N.Y 2010) p 292

16 Seminar organized by CSR in February 2019. Mr Nafees Zadeh felt that due to peaceful rise of China the only way to unite the Western states is by developing East vs West narrative. He writes for several Persian news-papers.

17 Zhou Xin sheng and Zhou Young '21st Century global maritime strategic environment and naval development', *Journal of National Defense University*, no 11 (1999).

18 https://daydaynews.ce/en/international/in-the-1993-yinhe-incident-sha-zukang-repeatedly-said.html

19 Edward Chan, 'Growing as a Sea Power: Development of China's Maritime Security Strategy from Deng Xiaoping to Xi Jinping' (1978-2018), January 2020 pp 191-192 https://ses.library.usyd.edu.au/handle/2123/21753

20 Ibid P 193.

21 China's National Defense in the New Era, July 2019 https://english.socio.gov.cn/m/2019-07/24content-75026800-5.htm p3

22 Hasan Yaser Malik, 'The Emerging Strategic Rivalries in Indian Ocean Region: An Analysis of Indo-American Ambitions and Implications for China', *Journal of Contemporary Studies*, Vol III, No 2, Winter 2014 p.78.

23 Sohni Bose, 'The Chittagong Port: Bangladesh's trump card in its diplomacy of Balance', 17 May 2022, www.orfonline.org

24 Kiran Stacy, 'China Signs 99 year lease on Sri Lanka's Hambantota port', Financial Times, 11 December 2017.

25 Details are given in chapter dealing with Gwadar.

26 Soren Scholvin, FIIA working paper April 2016, 'Geopolitics an Overview of Concepts and Empirical Examples from International Relations'. The Finish Institute of International Affairs, p10

27 It amounted to 3.4 trillion $ in 2016 according to China Power 'How Much Trade Transits the South China Sea'. http://chinapower.CSIS.org

28 Marina Tsirbas, *The Diplomat* 2 June 2016

29 Liu Zhen 12 July 2016

30 Hannah Beach, Shanghai 19 July 2016.

31 Taisaku Ikeshima 'China's Dash Line in South China Sea: Legal limits and Future Prospects', CORE, Waseda Global Forum No10, 2013

32 Wang (Faculty Nanjing University) Reported by Hannah Beech, Shanghai 19 July 2016.

33 Jeffrey A. Bader 'The US and China's 9-Dash Line: Ending the Ambiguity', 6 February 2018 Brooking.

34 Hannah Beech, Shanghai, 19 July 2016.

35 China to develop Arctic shipping routes opened by global warming http://www.bbc.com/news/world-asia-china-42833178

36 China to push for building 'Polar Silk Road' in Arctic Ocean https://www.business.standard.com/article/international/china-to-push-for-building-

polar-silk-road-in-arctic-ocean121030500701-1.html

37 Currently it takes 48 days to reach Rotterdam from China passing through Strait of Malacca and Suez Canal. Under the Arctic scheme the travel time will be reduced by three weeks.

38 China's 'Arctic Silk Road' https://www.maritime-executive.com/editorials/china-s-arctic-silk-road#;~text=Thr%20worlds%20largest%20 liquified%20natural,joint%20Arctic%20silk%20 road%20venture.

39 China's Arctic Silk Road https://www.maritime-executive

40 Ibid.

41 Ibid

42 During the Cold War, Egypt Syria, Iraq (after the socialist revolution) and Yemen established close relations with Soviet Union.

43 The US military base in Diego Garcia is still under US control and can be used to launch wars of aggression by the US in future as well.

44 Richard Weitz, 'Pivot Out, Rebalance In', *The Diplomat* 3 May 2012. According to Weitz the prevailing approach of US strategists attending the US Army War College Conference on Security, Asia will remain a major focus of US. The idea is to contain China. Also read John Ford 'The Pivot to Asia was Obama's Biggest mistake', *The Diplomat* 21 January 2017.

45 Van Jackson, 'America's Indo-Pacific Folly Adding New Commitments in Asia Will only Invite Disaster,' *Foreign Affairs*, 12 March 2021, www.foreignaffairs.com

46 Robert D. Kaplan, Opcit.

47 Van Jackson, Opcit.

48 According to Mr Shepovalenko (retired from

Russian navy) Quad suffers from a number of problems which might reduce its effectiveness in future. He presented a paper at Bahria University (Karachi, Pakistan) seminar.

49 Ambassador (Retired) Syed Hasan Javed who has written several books on China, also held important diplomatic positions in China threw light on this dimension in my interview with him.

50 Ambassador (Retired) G. Rasool Baluch, 'The Quad Chariot and the New Great Game in Indo-Pacific'. E paper 13 April 2021

51 US organized naval exercises in SCS are often provocative as they enter Chinese territorial waters without seeking prior permission. www.forbes.com

52 Dr Claude Rakisits Honrary Associate Professor in International Relations, Australia National University of Queensland.

53 Rear Admiral (Retired) Pervaiz Asghar (PN) currently working at Bahria University (Karachi) Also served as Director General National Centre for Maritime Policy Research.

54 Vice Admiral (Retired) Asaf Humayun is of the view that US avoids fighting wars against strong states. According to him there is no possibility of a military tilt led by China for another twenty five years.

55 Professor Luigi Troiani, Pontifical University Angelicum, Rome.

56 In his farewell speech, President Eisenhower warned against growing influence of military-industrial complex 17 January 1961. Also see *Global Times* article by Hu Yuwel and Lu Yameng which outlined growing influence of US military-industrial complex. According to them US aggression against Afghanistan was a blunder but it served the financial interest of military-industrial complex.

57 Australia cancelled a multi-billion dollar deal with

France to build a fleet of submarines.
https://reuters.com/business/cop/french-ambassador-accuses-australia-of-deceit-over-submarine-deal-2021-11-03/

58 Is AUKUS the New ASEAN in the Indo-Pacific?
    Anubha Gupta 9 May 2022 www.orfonline.org

59 New Zealand has declared that it will not allow
    nuclear powered vessels to call on its civil and
    naval facilities. When Five Eyes gave statements
    against China, New Zealand refused to join.

60 Five Eyes, Nine Eyes and Fourteen Eyes is in the
    process of expanding further, Japan, Singapore,
    South Korea and a few other nations are reported to
    be interested in joining the group. Zen Bahar 'How
    the Five Eyes alliance fuels global surveillance'
    21 April 2022, Nord VPN. Also see Frank Gardner
    (BBC security correspondent) 'Five Eyes: Is the
    alliance in trouble over China', 4 May 2021.

61 Robert D. Kaplan, Opcit p221

62 Port Muhammad Bin Qasim

63 15th February 2023 Dawn.com

64 A book written by K.M. Panikkar, *India and the Indian
    Ocean,* in 1945. It is suggested that India should
    be the dominant power in the Indian Ocean. This
    constitutes the Indian naval strategy in the twenty
    first Century. Also see 'India's "Grand Strategy" for
    the Indian Ocean: Mahanian visions' David A. Scott
    article in *Asia Pacific Review* November 2006 vol 13,
    No2 pp104-110

65 David A. Scott, Ibid p107. Scott has quoted Panikkar
    in his article printed in *Asia Pacific Review*.

66 Sanat Kaur, 'Andaman and Nicobar Island', https://
    idsa.in>files>book

67 Indian control over Nicobar and Andaman give it
    definite advantage in the Strait of Malacca.

68 Bidanda Chengappa, 'India's island diplomacy

gains momentum' The Hindu business Line www.thehindubusinessline.com

69 China says it has signed pact with Solomon Islands Aljazeera 19 April 2022 https://www.aljazeera.com/news/2022/4/19/ china-says-it-has-signed-security-pact-with-solomon-islands.

70 Zongyuan Zee Liu CFR Expert, 4 May 2022, Council on Foreign Relations. https://cfr.org/in-brief/china-solomon-islands-security-pact-us-south-pacific.

CONCLUSION

According to Chinese proverb a journey of a thousand miles begins by taking the first step. Belt and Road Initiative of which CPEC is a flagship project, is the first step of a long journey which is expected to promote cooperation and end poverty. In recent history two major projects were launched by Western nations. Marshall plan was launched by the US soon after World War II for the purpose of rebuilding Europe. The war shattered economies of European states were to be revived. US succeeded in its endeavours. Europe which had been ruined as a result of the war was rebuilt and European states were able to strengthen their economies. However, it was a programme which was restricted to Europe and was therefore much narrower in scope. Another factor which seems significant is related to Cold War. The US was in need of allies and Marshall Plan provided the mechanism to achieve that objective. US has never launched this kind of programme anywhere in the developing world.

The second major step was taken by European states themselves towards integration, where by European Economic Community culminated into

European Union within few decades. This was also very limited in its scope. Developing states were not to benefit from this scheme of integration. If anything, this club of developed states has further eroded, the ability of developing states to negotiate and acquire good terms of trade.

For the first time developing states have a common platform in the form of BRI. The project has tremendous scope as it is not limited to any one region. Asia, Europe, Africa and other regions can gain by joining the BRI. For the first time developed and developing states have a common platform for mutual cooperation without trying to dominate each other.

There is a lot of enthusiasm and euphoria surrounding BRI particularly in the third world which is quite understandable. However, we should not lose sight of the challenges which have emerged or could arise in future. Challenges can be natural or manmade; in either case strategies have to be devised to confront them effectively.

More than sixty-five states have already joined BRI and many others are exploring the pros and cons of joining the venture. The number of states participating in BRI is expected to grow in future. All these are sovereign states, having different cultures and adhering to different political systems. Their work ethics and operational mechanisms vary. Under these circumstances it should not come as a surprise, if problems of coordination and delays in implementation of projects take place. In order to redress this problem workshops bringing relevant stake holders together might be a good idea. Exposure to different methods of doing work, learning from each other's experiences and coordinating policy measures would be beneficial for all the parties.

Another factor which could hold back progress of BRI is diverse historical backgrounds of states participating in the venture. Some states have joined because of expectations of gain, but they continue to have misgivings about some other member states of BRI. At some stage BRI would need support from Think Tanks already existing in countries associated with BRI. If this frame-work is weak it will have to be strengthened. Special research centres focusing particularly on BRI related issues are need of the hour. Under CPEC cooperation between Chinese and Pakistani universities is envisaged. This frame-work could be expanded to include selected universities from other BRI countries. Crisis management mechanisms and institutions will also need to be developed. States could have recourse to these institutions in case of a dispute. Since UN has failed in its function of crisis management and conflict resolution, there is a wide gap which cannot be left open for adversaries to exploit.

India's animosity towards BRI springs from its opposition to China. It wants infrastructure projects under its own leadership but lacks the financial and other resurces to launch them. US opposition to BRI is the result of its Cold War mentality. There is also an assumption that the success of BRI would further enhance China's influence. The US is fearful of increase in China's influence, as it is aware of decline in its own standing in the developing world. There is no easy solution to this problem, but one can expect improvement in the prevailing situation. This could happen as a result of cumulative effect of other developments in world politics. At present there is no sign of improvement, if anything the opposite trend seems to be dominant.

Propaganda against BRI and CPEC is at its peak. US think tanks have focused on the 'debt trap'. There is exaggeration and some concoctions are also visible.

Dawn (Karachi) dated 24th February 2023 has highlighted India's disinfo drive specifically against Pakistan and China. An Indian news agency by the name of Asian News International (ANI) has been playing central role in this media compaign. Ghost experts are regularly quoted by ANI. 'Non-existent' think tanks have also been mentioned prominently in anti-Pakistan and anti-China compaigns launched by India. Since investigations have revealed that 'experts' and 'think tanks' are fake ANI stands exposed, its credibility has also been dented. European Union discovered a similar Indian campaign against Pakistan in 2019-2022. The disinfo lab operating from Europe was used by India for several decades, finally being exposed when they quoted a European professor who had died many years back. This discovery led to an investigation by European Union.

The interesting point is that India has not been discouraged, it continues with its disinfo Campaigns against its adversaries. Even though crudely managed Indian efforts have not entirely failed. The same tools eg social media, print and electronic media are available to Pakistan, China and other countries to debunk Indian propaganda. We should learn from Indian failures in order to make our counter campaign more credible and ethical. The decision whether counter campaign should be defensive, offensive or a combination of the two, will have to be made keeping all aspects of the situation in mind. One thing is clear that Pakistan and China cannot afford to lose the media war, India and other states propaganda has to be dispelled.

Another dimension which is being used by the US to dissuade states from becoming part of BRI is economic in nature. Financial pressure is being applied through IMF and World Bank. Pakistan which has been made dependent on IMF through the intrigues of local economic hitmen and the US is facing adverse consequences. The main target of IMF appears to be Pakistan's participation in CPEC. The possibility of ending Pakistan's dependance on IMF through CPEC, is not acceptable to those who want to see Pakistan on the crutches. These pressure tactics could be used by IMF to target other states as well. China has created two institutions in the form of AIIB and SRF to promote projects related to BRI. Other institutions could be created to contain the influence of IMF and World Bank. The West continues to rule over the developing states through Bretton Wood and other institutions but this has to change.

The US is known for its covert operations all over the world. Leaders who refused to tow the US policy have been victims of regime change policy. Some were toppled or even assassinated, their countries had to go through turmoil and civil war. Libya has disintegrated, Syria and Iraq are still suffering due to US covert operations. In many cases overt US military intervention also took place but most of these occurred in South America. Afghanistan and Iraq also suffered overt US aggression, but according to many experts I interviewed, US avoids direct military confrontation against strong states. In the case of Russia it tried to use Ukraine instead of directly attacking Russia. In my opinion US will not attack China or Pakistan directly but that does not mean that it will give up its opposition to BRI.

Biological weapons are now within the reach of many nations but US Bioweapons programme is most developed. Probably due to this reason, when Covid 19 broke out in China, many people including experts believed that some adversary of China could be involved. The UN should inspect

Biolabs on US soil and also overseas. US had established Biolabs in Ukraine and several other states. China, Russia and developing states, should launch a movement against Bioweapons to make the world safe.

Initially the US tried to pin the blame on China when Covid-19 broke out. A 'classified' intelligence report prepared by the US Energy Department is quite revealing. Under this China has been cleared of any complicity in spreading Covid-19. According to the report covered by Dawn (27th February 2023) Covid-19 could be the result of laboratory leak. This is bad news for countries hosting US or any other Bioweapon labs. They could be adversely affected in case of another leak from one of these labs.

HAARP United States Climate Control programme has also been subject of discussion for a number of years. Perhaps climate control programmes would not have evoked concern, had they been used to tame the weather for common good. The source of concern is perceived US desire to undermine the interests of its adversaries through the control of their climate. Some recent developments in the field of climate control carry serious implications for the future. When one state acquires the ability to manipulate climate, others would like to do the same in order to protect themselves. The possibility of US using HAARP to undermine BRI, or any other state using it for some other objective is fraught with danger. A global commission, composed of peace oriented technologically advanced states, should be formed to keep strict control over the situation. It will happen only after several states acquire the capability to control climate not in the absence of that.

The member states of BRI should not take these threats lightly. They should launch a global movement against Bioweapons, and Climate Control programmes, within the UN and also carry the concept, to other global and regional organisations.

There has been a major paradigm shift in US policy. Geopolitics and geoeconomics are clearly reflected in this new approach. Indo-Pacific policy shifted the focus of US from Europe to India and East Asia. Now Central Asia is also gaining greater prominence. Ever since the independence of Central Asian States, US wanted to eliminate Russian influence from the region but it faced setbacks at every stage. The US did not give up its ambitions but rather adopted wait and see approach. The launching of BRI, however, appears to have given fresh impetus to US interest in the region.

The US policy makers realise the importance of Central Asia and South Asia (particularly Pakistan) in the context of BRI. US Secretary of State Antony J. Blinken has spelt out main features of US approach. The US has already launched a full-fledged scheme to create a divide between Central Asia,

Russia and China. The narrative being developed is, that Russia poses a military threat to Central Asia and, US could be the only source of security to the region. In reality however, US has been a source of threat to more developing states than any other major power. In recent times US launched 81 percent of wars against developing states. Among victims of US aggression resource rich states constitute the majority. This too does not auger well for Central Asian Republics (CARS).

China, Russia, CARs, Pakistan, Afghanistan, Iran and Turkiye in spite of some inherent contradictions stand to gain from BRI. They can visualise the benefits, which would go a long way, in improving the standard of living of people in the region. With improvement in economic condition there could be expectations of greater political stability. People learn from experience and cooperation becomes a habit, when people experience benefits due to mutual interdependence and cooperation. China, Russia Pakistan and other countries should increase coordination in their policies. BRI is too precious for us to allow US or any other country to play with the future of more than 3 billion people.

Recently a seminar was organized by Pakistan Institute of International Affairs (PIIA). The subject was Hybrid Warfare and its implications for Pakistan. It is true that in the last few years Pakistan has suffered from a combination of tools used against it. Terrorism sponsored by some states destroyed Pakistan's economy and political stability. Sanctions against Pakistan and other states are another tool, which is being used to undermine target states economy. The tools being used against Pakistan can be used against other developing and developed states. The crucial question we face today is whether something can be done to redress the situation?

BRI members should devise their own strategy to meet the challenges being posed to them. This could be done at national level but in my opinion coordination with other BRI members would be more helpful. Another relevant move would be integration of intelligence gathering networks. In this regard much can be learnt from the West. Four-Eyes developed into Nine-Eyes which has now become Fourteen-Eyes. It brought together Western states along with their allies, to pool their resources for the purpose of intelligence gathering. Without reliable knowledge derived from intelligence sources both human and artificial effective security mechanisms cannot be developed.

China's role in helping Iran and Saudi Arabia to overcome their differences has enhanced China's growing role in world politics. China is signing deals with other countries which are not based on dollar; yuan or the other trading partner's currency will be used. This will impact global economic system, reducing the value of dollar and, creating greater space or Chinese and other currencies. China's expanding role in economic and political spheres will be consolidated. If member states are able to follow up these developments with other cooperative measures in future, it will strengthen BRI

The concept of 'shared prosperity' floated by China in recent times has kindled hopes of a prosperous future among people of developing states. There is hope which has to be nurtured and kept alive at every cost. Those who consider it to be no more than a dream will ultimately realise, that when people start believing in a dream and become driving force behind it, it becomes reality.